THE IRON MILLS
AT CRAMOND

E.U.E.A. STUDIES IN LOCAL HISTORY

Previously published:

The Lime Industry in the Lothians
The Mapping of a Scottish Estate
Royal Visit of 1822
Corstorphine on the Night of 6th June 1841

THE IRON MILLS
AT CRAMOND

Patrick Cadell, B.A.

BRATTON PUBLISHING LIMITED

FOR

UNIVERSITY OF EDINBURGH
EXTRA-MURAL STUDIES

1973

Published by Bratton Publishing Limited
35 Moray Place
Edinburgh EH3 6BX

ISBN 0 85975 001 9

Typesetting by Speedspools, Edinburgh
Printed in Great Britain by Peridon Ltd, Stanmore, Middlesex

CONTENTS

Foreword   vii
1. Early Days under Carron   1
2. The Cadell Period   9
3. The Final Phase of the Mills   29
4. The Mill Sites   37
    Notes and References   41

APPENDICES

1. Cramond in 1782   45
2. Cramond in 1803   47
3. Cramond in 1855   49
4. Workmen employed at Cramond Iron Works 1767   54
5. Workmen at Cramond 1792, 1841, 1851, 1861   55
6. Details of Population of Cramond in 1792   64
7. Remarks on Expenses of Cramond 1765-6   65
8. Expenses of Cramond 1766   68
9. Supply of Iron 1778   69
10. Technical Terms used by the Company 1778   70
11. Letter reporting Supply of Iron from Russia 1804   72
12. Profit and Loss at Cramond 1847-60   74
13. Legal Dispatches involving Cramond Iron Works 1774-1852   77
14. Participants in the Research   83
15. Cadell Family Tree   84

FOREWORD

Mr Cadell's study of the Cramond iron works is an expansion of the work done by an extra-mural class of Edinburgh University in 1965 under Mr B. C. Skinner. This new research was conducted by another class in 1969-70. Much new material, largely from the Cadell family papers and not available to Mr Skinner, was examined.

Mr Cadell had three purposes in his enquiry, to examine the operations at Cramond in its heyday from about 1770 to about 1790 when Cramond was a place to visit, to give some reasons for the decline of Cramond and to sketch the brief revival in the nineteenth century. If the record seems incomplete or patchy so indeed is the surviving evidence. In the appendices are a number of interesting documents and statistics hitherto unpublished or not readily available.

The Edinburgh University Extra-Mural Association is happy to make this research available in this publication.

J. B. BARCLAY
Extra-Mural Studies, University of Edinburgh

CHAPTER I

EARLY DAYS UNDER CARRON

The River Almond between Cramond Brig and the sea was an ideal spot in pre-Industrial Revolution terms for milling. There was a steep fall on the river, good farm land on either side, and the sea at the river mouth permitted easy access from places outside the immediate neighbourhood.

There were five mills on the Almond between the bridge and the sea. The highest was Dowie's Mill on the east bank of the river just below the bridge (and sometimes referred to as the Bridge Mill). The origin of this name is uncertain but it has been suggested that it comes from 'Davie' Strachan who was one of the partners in the Smith and Wright Work Company of Leith and who at one time owned and perhaps operated the mill. Next below on the same side is Peggie's Mill or Peggy's Mill or Pigas Mill or even Piggies Mill. This name may possibly derive from the 'pickieman' who was a mill servant responsible for the upkeep of the mill machinery.

These two mills are referred to in a charter of 1697 by which they were acquired by John Menzies of Cammo and in which they are described respectively as the 'Old' and 'New' Mills. In 1699 Menzies bought Whitehouse from John Corse whose father, James, had bought it from the Primrose family, and the mills were then united to that estate. Menzies sold Whitehouse to his son-in-law, George Adie, W.S. in 1719. Adie died in 1750 and the property was sold in May of that year to David Strachan. The lands were then bought in 1776 by Lady Glenorchy from Strachan's son and the two mills passed from her to the Cadell family, Peggie's Mill in 1781, Dowie's in 1782.

The next mill on the river, this time on the west side, is Craigie Mill. This mill, built on the one flat piece of ground on that side of the river, was the only mill on the Dalmeny estate. On the whole it does not seem to have done well. Archibald Lunn who occupied Craigie Mill in 1703 had a feu of Peggie's Mill from Menzies of Cammo and may therefore have been of some substance. By 1740 Craigie Mill was in a state of decay and though the house was occupied into the nineteenth century the mill had been idle for many years. These three mills were all originally grain mills. Fairafar the next mill on the east side was also a waukmill. It is mentioned for the first time in 1676. The origin of the name is unknown.

The lowest mill, at the highest reach of the tide, Cockle Mill, was a grain mill, as its name suggests, for cockle is a kind of weed that grows in corn crops. In East Lothian to this day the whole crop when cut and before the removal of any weeds is known as cockle. It has been alleged by an old inhabitant of Cramond that in his own memory cockle shells from Cramond Island were crushed at Cockle Mill for use as farm fertiliser. There seems to be no evidence that this ever took place at the mill after 1752. Any 'memory' must be a village tradition.

This mill, known originally as Cramond Mill, is first recorded in 1178 when it was a possession of the abbot of Inchcolm who derived an annual rent of four merks from it.[1] The *molendinum de Crawmond cum terris molendinariis et multuris* (the mill at Cramond with its mill lands and dues) remained a perquisite of the abbey and latterly of the Earls of Moray, as commendators, until 1628.[2] In 1643 the mill belonged to Sir Patrick Hamilton of Little Preston, but sometime later it came into the hands of the Inglis family who had been established in the area since 1622. Cramond Mill, however, seems to have been somehow under the control of the lairds of Whitehouse from at least 1615, when it is mentioned in a charter to David Primrose, advocate. It may be that Hamilton of Little Preston kept only the superiority of the mill and that the owners of Whitehouse feued it from him. Certainly the mill appears to have been included in Whitehouse estate up to the beginning of the eighteenth century.

It is possible fairly precisely to date the origin of industrial iron-working at Cramond. A contract of feu drawn up on 23 July 1752,[3] between Sir John Inglis of Cramond on the one hand and the co-partners of the Smith and Wright Work Company of Leith on the other makes reference to 'the nethermost mill next to the sea upon the Water of Cramond, commonly called the Cockle Mill, and which was formerly used as a Corn Mill, but is now converted into an Iron splitting mill by the said Company'. From this it is clear that the installation of a furnace and of iron rolling and slitting machinery driven from the water wheel of the old mill must have taken place at Cockle Mill not long before the year 1752. The same feu contract also includes 'Sir John Inglis' mill called Fairyfare . . . with the mill lead

2

for conveying water thereto, and Kilne'. This mill was still referred to in 1759 as 'consisting of a meal mill and a waulkmill'.

It would seem therefore that the initial industrial development was confined to Cockle Mill and that Fairafar continued to serve the needs of local farmers and weavers. The mention of a waukmill at Fairafar is interesting for another reason. In the feu contract of 1752, both mills were referred to as 'formerly possesst by James Macdowall', an Edinburgh merchant whose name appeared on the roll of co-partners of the Smith and Wright Work Company. This was James Macdowall of Canonmills (d. 1786), son of Patrick Macdowall, the merchant banker, and father of Archibald Macdowall (1742-1816). Archibald was to establish a reputation as a pioneer cloth manufacturer in Scotland, operating at Paul's Work in Lower Calton and at Brunstane Mill, Portobello.[4] James Macdowall's wife was Lilias Warden, daughter of the minister of Cargunnock. Their daughter married her cousin John Warden or McFarlan who was minister of the Canongate. The connection between the Macdowalls of the Cramond mills and the family of Warden was possibly significant since a James Warden was recorded as tenant of Strachan's Mill in November 1756. David Strachan who has already been mentioned was also a partner in the company. Not only did he have interests in Cramond already, he was also a burgess in Edinburgh and a merchant in Leith. It is thought that he was probably not connected with John Strachan of Craigcrook (d. 1719) whose mortification is quoted in great detail in Wood's *Parish of Cramond*.

Two of the partners of the Smith and Wright Work Company of Leith were thus fully identified as having territorial interests in Cramond. The remainder were James Mansfield (d. 1753), William Hogg (d. 1767), Thomas Hogg, John Forrest, James Grant, John Walker, William Neilson (d. 1771), and John Stephen, all described as merchants in Edinburgh. John Dick (d. 1774) was a shipmaster in Leith, James Campbell, a sea-captain, Alexander Chalmers (d. 1760) accountant at the Excise Office in Edinburgh and Jeremy Pew who was admitted as an additional partner in 1751 son of John Pew, farmer, at Newmains or Laugh-at-Leith. Of these only John Walker needs further introduction. He is perhaps identical with Bailie John Walker who, for some years after the establishment of the Carron Company, enjoyed milling rights at the slit mill on certain days each week. Perhaps he was the owner of Walker's Mill further up the river near Leny.

The company had been founded in 1747 by William Moyes, a wright in Leith, for the manufacture of small forgings, wheels, carts and ploughs. The company became well known for its products but Moyes did not seem to have been very skilful in business and the works were taken over by the larger partnership in November 1749. From then the company went over exclusively to iron products and planned to import its own bar iron. It was with this in mind that they leased the two lower mills at Cramond in 1752. Their main product seems to have been, as it was later for the Carron Company, rod iron for manufacture of nails but they also made a large selection of small items such as spades, hoes, chains, anchors, traps and tools of all sorts.

If their works were of no great extent compared with later developments, they were of great importance as a pioneering industrial concern. The company had selected the site of the present dam at Cockle Mill and it is possible that the dock at the mill may have been constructed by them.

On 21 December 1759, the company sold their mills at Cramond, 'the slitmill and blade-mill formerly called Cockle Mill', and 'Fairyfare Mill', by public roup in St John's Coffee House in Parliament Close, a well-known venue for auction sales over several generations. The judge of the sale was a Mr James Russell, surgeon, and the properties were offered together at a starting price of £1000. There being only one bid of £1010 the two mills were knocked down at this figure to Dr John Roebuck.

With Dr Roebuck's purchase, Carron Company came to Cramond. The annals of the company in its more general progress have been so well recounted already that it is only necessary to summarise here the main points of significance.[5] The deed of agreement that led to the foundation of Carron Company was signed early in 1760, although back-dated to 11 November 1759. The original partners were Dr John Roebuck, inventor and scientist, from Birmingham, Samuel Garbett, Birmingham industrialist, William Cadell sen. (1708-77), of Cockenzie, merchant and manufacturer, his son William Cadell jun. (1737-1819), who became the first general manager of the company, and three other members of Roebuck's family. To these were added at a later stage a number of other partners of whom perhaps the most important was Charles Gascoigne, Garbett's son-in-law, who succeeded William Cadell jun. as manager, and who was at least partly responsible for the withdrawal of the Cadell family from the company.

4

As early as February 1759 the partners had started looking for a site for a major iron works in Scotland. Various sites were considered including Haddington, Seton, Bo'ness and Monymusk, but by agreement of 13 December 1759 the site at Carron was confirmed and building began. The first air-furnace was completed in March 1760, while the first of the blast furnaces went into production on Boxing Day of the same year and the second in September 1761.

It will be seen therefore that the purchase of the Cramond mills in December 1759, complete with equipment and, presumably, good-will, not only presented Carron Company with their first operative mills in Scotland but also provided business during the crucial eighteen months of development at the main works at Carron. Writing to the Cadells in February 1760, however, Garbett remarked, 'It's my opinion that we should not lock up a large sum of money in that work (Cramond) untill we have Iron of our own, as the profits will be very small.'

That production at Cramond continued uninterrupted from the Leith Company's days into the Carron period can be deduced from one clause in the deed of sale. By this it was provided that the contracts of employment of John Lee (or Leigh) and his son Richard as principal hands at the mills should be continued for at least six months after the sale. It was important that the mills should be kept going as Garbett said in the letter already quoted, 'Let Lee at the Slit Mill go on in his own way if he is not very unreasonable untill I see him. He may in many respects be of great use to us. He hath acquaintance amongst fordgemen which we shall find it difficult to obtain.' But the Lees soon proved idle and careless and had to be removed at the end of 1760.[6]

As early as 10 January 1760, William Cadell wrote to James Dunlop, the Glasgow merchant, saying, 'The Company . . . having purchast the slitt Miln on Cramond if you or any of your friends want any Iron Slitt or Rolld they may get it done on reasonable terms'.[7] Regular reports throughout the spring and summer of 1760 showed the slitmill in as constant production as the uncertain water supply allowed.

Though Cramond was of great importance to Carron Company during its early stages, its value to the parent company waned in proportion as the great blast furnaces and forges at Carron reached full production. By 1761, the slitmill was reckoned to account for only 15 per cent of all Carron expenditure while its profits were even less, just 12 per cent of all Carron revenue. Two years later the mill was shown as a mere 9 per cent of Carron's total capital investment. These figures by no means imply that Cramond was in decline. The value of the mill, bought in December 1759 for £1010, was assessed at least on paper at £1411 in 1761 and at £3075 in 1766. It was developing all the time but development at Carron was always faster and more profitable. It is not surprising, therefore, that, with Gascoigne as manager, the parent company was happy to rid itself of Cramond in October 1770 when William Cadell jun. bought the mill and the company's nail trade.

Carron Company's rule at Cramond was thus from December 1759 to the autumn of 1770. During that period four managers represented the company's interests on the spot. First there was John Lee already mentioned. He was replaced at the end of 1760 by James Alexander who later went to be the company's representative at Dunfermline and who was himself replaced on 31 July 1761 by John Simpson.

The degree of responsibility enjoyed by these managers seems to have varied. Lee in Leith Company days was apparently a semi-independent agent, prepared to find his own 'coal, soap, and candles'. Carron Company, however, through the younger Cadell and Gascoigne, maintained the closest surveillance on the conduct of the mills and had no hesitation in writing hectoring letters of criticism to their men at Cramond.

Later a more conciliatory tone can be detected. A long letter of instructions issued on Simpson's appointment throws interesting light on this system of control. By each post, three times a week, the manager had to send to Carron a report of every occurrence at the mill, a copy of every inward or outward message, a full account of all work done with explanation of any shortcomings, and a name list of any visitors shown round the works.

As far as the workmen were concerned Simpson was 'never to keep any person an hour longer than he's really useful', never to re-employ men who had left the service without just cause, and to forbid any of the company's employees to sell or dispense alcohol. This last direction (which was a standing order at the Cadells' colliery at Grange) was to be read specifically to the master slitter, Christopher Bell. 'Fidelity and activity', wrote William Cadell, 'are what we require, and if you show these in a proper degree you may depend upon all reasonable encouragement from us.'[8]

Carron Company's system of direct supervision seems on the whole to have been successful in detecting inefficiency among the staff, but Simpson himself was soon in trouble. Letters from Cadell to the slit mill were full of complaints. Simpson's monthly accounts were submitted late. Orders were confused and rod iron of the wrong size was shipped to merchants in England. 'You have sent to Leith for Messrs Gabril & Hall & Co. of Newcastle', Simpson was told on 26 July 1764, '$1\frac{1}{2}$ ton Rod Iron which should have been sent for Mattison and Morrison at Alnick. . . . We should be glad to know how the mistake occurred.'

It is on the whole surprising that Simpson's period of office lasted its three years. In February 1765 he was replaced by a man who was to become an important figure in Scottish iron-making history, Thomas Edington. He took Edington's place again for a short while in 1766 when Edington was on a study trip to some English iron works.

In contrast with the 615 employees at Carron, in 1761 at Cramond, apart from the manager and his clerk, the operative labour force at the slitmill was remarkably small (see Appendix 4). Cadell wrote in 1762 that Bell and his son and three hands should manage the works among them. Christopher Bell was for some years the master-slitter and the number of men for normal shiftworking seems to have been not more than four or five. It varied, however, with the amount of water in the river. 'When water is plentiful you might hire 1 or 2 more hands and go double shift', was one instruction, but in February 1766, always a period of the year of outstanding production, the manager was enjoined to 'carry on night and day with 6 hands'. At other times as in summer when water was very short workmen were freely dismissed as soon as their work became redundant.

Christopher Bell was undoubtedly a man of some importance at the mill. When Edington took up his appointment in 1765 he was warned 'not to do anything that will lessen his (Bell's) consequence as principal workman'. Indeed upon the slitter's skill much of the profit of the mill depended.

In 1762 some thought was given to his conditions of employment and information was sought from other mills as to their wage rates. At one a master workman was paid 10s a week and found his own firing and paid rent for his house. At the Smithfield Company in Glasgow, a mill twenty years older than Cramond, the slitter found his own coals and house and maintained his own tools, while the company provided grease and candles and paid him two guineas towards each new pair of cutters.

Carron Company eventually adopted the same piece rate system as that in operation in the Durham slitmills, paying Bell 5s a ton from which he paid all wages, and obliging him to produce a ton of rod iron for every 21 cwt of bar iron supplied to him, with an allowance of one shilling for every cwt of rod iron produced above this figure. 'This makes him Heat slit and bundle his Iron with the greatest exactness.' This rate was quite generous as it allowed a theoretical 5 per cent wastage of iron while it was generally considered at this period that a 3 per cent wastage was what iron masters should expect. That was not really a possibility at Cramond for reasons given in the next chapter. In 1762 Bell was sent on a study tour to the Smithfield Company to look at their work methods.

Despite the reliance placed upon him by the company Bell in the end had to go. In 1764 as well as in 1762 he had been warned against selling ale at the mill 'which we consider a very bad thing for the workmen'. By 1765 Bell's 'bungling' had cost the company a new set of rollers. On 1 July 1767 he was dismissed with five guineas compensation and the company's representative was to 'endeavour to engage a Compleat slitter' to take over. By November 1767 the slitter was Joshua Padmore. Bell subsequently went to Peggie's Mill of which he is described as tenant in the Cramond baptismal register of 1768.

In the whole period of Carron Company's management at Cramond, there is no reason to suppose that their works extended beyond the slit mill at Cockle Mill which they took over from the Leith Company. In all records, references are to the 'mill' or to 'the Damheid' and there is no sign that Fairafar Mill was developed for iron-making before 1770. The company was so far from expanding that the co-partners did in fact refuse an offer in 1761 from Lord Rosebery of Craigie Mill. The end of Carron Company's ownership at Cramond came in 1770. In the opinion of the parent company Cramond had outlived its usefulness and its low profitability and irregular production made it something of a liability. The Cadell family, however, were more interested in a wide variety of small businesses than in one large one and were therefore happy to take over the Cramond concern.

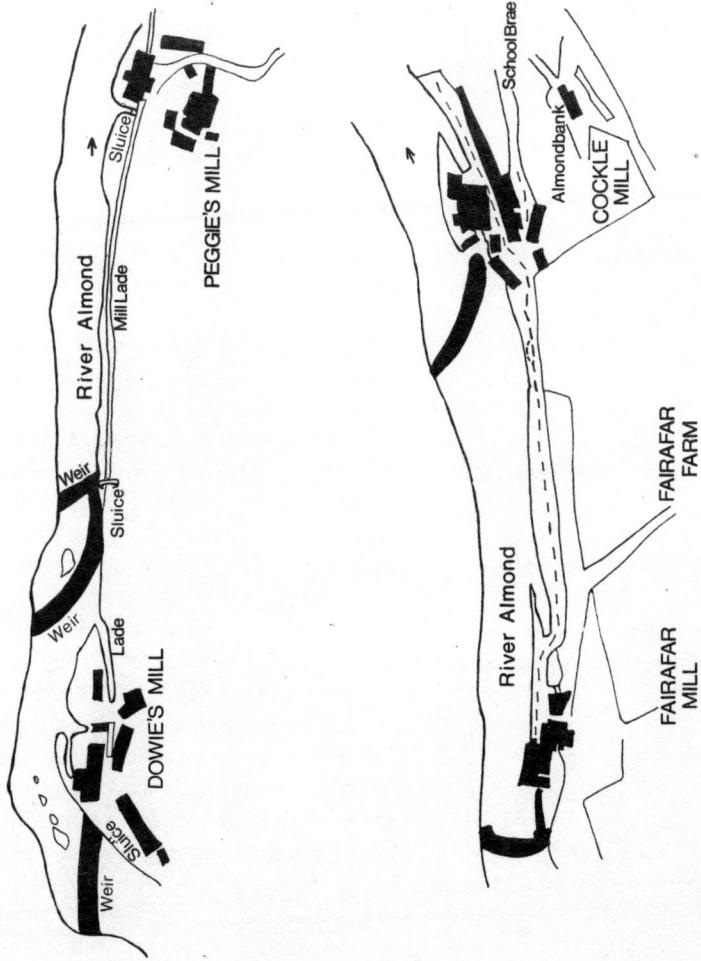

Plate 1 *Top* Location of buildings at Peggie's and Dowie's Mills in 1890s
Bottom Location of buildings at Cockle and Fairafar Mills from Thomas Carfrae's
map, 1839

Plate 2 *Cockle Mill* taken in 1895

A view of the mill-workers' houses and the three-storied office building with the dock in the foreground. A winch or gin, possibly horse-operated, can be seen to the right

CHAPTER 2

THE CADELL PERIOD

In 1773 William Cadell wrote to Sir William Forbes, the banker, from whom he hoped to obtain credit facilities. He described how the Cadell family had acquired the Cramond works: 'In October 1770 we purchased from Carron Compy their slitting & Rolling Mill at Crammond, with the nail trade at Crammond and in the neighbourhood of Carron for which we paid £4839:14:2 in Carron Stock. At same time we bought their stock of Barr Iron, Iron Hoops, Rod Iron, Nails for which we paid £10585:2:1 in Money being their primecost.' 'We have since added to these works a Furnace for converting Barr Iron into Steel & a forge for drawing it into different purposes.'

The sum paid in Carron stock represented the last 1/26 share that William Cadell held in the company. The purchase was nothing more than a straightforward exchange, Carron being thankful to rid itself of a not very profitable concern, while Cadell was happy to leave on honourable terms a company which he thought was heading for bankruptcy.

THE CRAMOND WORKFORCE

In 1770 there were only two partners at Cramond, William Cadell himself and his younger brother John. Their father never seems to have had an interest there. The works continued to be managed by Thomas Edington who became a partner himself in 1772, the year in which he married the Cadells' sister Christian. Edington had started his career with Carron Company as a traveller about March 1764. He carried out sales duties in Northumberland and the south of Scotland and was evidently familiar with the slit mill at Bedlington near Morpeth. About a year after his appointment as manager at Cramond he was sent, in 1766, to study methods at what was probably the most important establishment of its kind in England and Cramond's chief rival, Crawley's Slitting Mills at Winlaton in Durham. He remained a partner at Cramond until about 1800, although from 1786 his main interests were elsewhere. From 1772 the principal clerk at Cramond was James Bathgate, son of the gardener at Craigiehall, who was to be of great assistance to J. P. Wood in the compilation of his *History of Cramond*. Both Edington and Bathgate were active men but both eventually left Cramond. There is no doubt that it was partly due to their energy and efficient management that a company which laboured under so many disadvantages was able to survive the various economic difficulties of the later eighteenth century.

Cramond employed other skilled craftsmen besides Christopher Bell and Joshua Padmore already mentioned. The most notable was undoubtedly Richard Squair, a Newcastle man, who was already at Cramond in 1780. He may well have come as early as Carron days with other imported English workmen. His skill in making spades and shovels gave Cramond a reputation in that branch of their business which long survived him. Though being 'old and not likely to live long', he was still with the firm in December 1798 when it was decided to appoint a new spademaker.

The rest of the labour force was small in the early days at Cramond. In 1762 it consisted only of Bell, his son, and three others. In November 1767, shortly after Bell's dismissal, the company employed eight people regularly, with three others in winter when there was plenty of water. They were a slitter (Joshua Padmore), paid 17s a week, his apprentice, a furnaceman, a middleman, a carpenter and cutterman, a hoop bundler who also made sad iron handles, and two general labourers, with a further furnaceman, middleman, and cutterman in winter. This gave a weekly wage bill of £2 17s, plus piecework rates for the hoop bundler (½d per hoop) and a further 18s for the three seasonal men.

By 1792, Cramond employed 12 millmen, 2 slitters, 2 carters, a carpenter, 6 forgemen, 8 labourers, 8 spademakers, 3 masons, 4 spade-shaft makers, 11 nailers and 22 boys (12 working at nails, 7 drawing and straightening hoops, 2 with the forgemen, and one an apprentice slitter), giving a grand total of 79. In 1810, Philip Cadell informed the kirk session that the workforce at Cramond would soon consist of almost ninety families. As more could be expected, something would have to be done to find them seating in the church.[9] By 1826, the year in which Lady Torphichen demolished a large part of Cramond village, the workforce was down to about thirty. In his *Parish of Cramond*, published in 1794 Wood says that there were 'above eighty men and

boys' employed at the works, a slight advance on the list given him by
Dr Robert Spotswood two years earlier.[10]

THE PRODUCTS AND OUTLETS

With the arrival of the Cadells at Cramond there began a period of
expansion. Fairafar Mill which had not previously been used for the
iron trade was in 1773 turned into the works forge where small forgings
such as files, plough socs, and girdles were made. The upper mills,
Peggie's and Dowie's, were bought in 1781 and 1782 respectively from
Lady Glenorchy. Dowie's Mill was used by the spademakers as their
workshop and included the sawmill which made the handles for the
spades. It was also occupied in 1826 by a colony of nailers. Peggie's Mill
was for a while used by the spademakers and even served for making
hoops before it became in 1815 the Cramond papermill.

One of the most important activities of the Cramond partners in the
years immediately after 1770 was that of securing new customers,
especially for nails and rod iron which were the largest items of production. Edington was particularly active in this field, travelling widely
over the country, visiting builders, dockyards and the Irish Ordnance
in Dublin. William Cadell preferred to operate from his desk but was
hardly less busy seeking orders. In 1774, he wrote to his lawyer John
Buchan who had influence with the Dundas family, 'The Fact is that
large Quantities of nails are used in the King's Yard, & no work can
supply them of a better Quality or upon easier terms than ourselves.
At Portsmouth . . . they use 6 or £8000 value yearly . . . the consumption at Deptford, Chatham & Plymouth must be proportionately
great. It would be of particular use to our Manufactory to serve them
to the amount of 2, 3, 4 or £5000 value yearly.'

The works were turning out about 300 tons of rod iron annually in
the 1760s and 1770s, of which about a third was made into nails, mostly
in the area of St Ninians, Camelon and Kilsyth, which all used Cramond
rod iron. Carron had succeeded in planting a colony of English nailers
in Stirlingshire as early as 1761. The English were less willing to come
to Cramond as there were no English there. Some nailers did settle in
Cramond after 1770. Half the nails made were sold locally, the other
half to London, Gosport or abroad.

The nail trade was clearly extremely refined. In April 1778 the list of types of nail available from Cramond was as follows: clasps and pounds for home sale, sharps for home and export, spriggs or brads for the London trade and export, Flemish, tobacco and sugar (specifically for sugar hogsheads) for coopers, flat pointed nails for America, clasp and deckheaded spikes, lighter nails, and sheathing nails for ships' carpenters, and a series of nails known as Quebec nails which included shallop, clap and scupper nails. Unfortunately, it is difficult to explain to-day exactly how these differed from each other.

The common varieties of nails were sold by the thousand at a certain weight per thousand. Thus spriggs, one of the commonest, could be obtained in various weights or sizes, from 3 lb per thousand to 20 lb per thousand, the price varying from 1s 6d per thousand for the 3 lb nails, to 5s 10d for the 20 lb nails, the relatively lower price for the latter reflecting the smaller amount of work required for their manu-facture. They were despatched in casks or in canvas bags procured from rope and sail makers in Leith.

A distinction was made which applied to all goods sold by Cramond between the price to ironmongers and the price to country dealers and exporters. Ironmongers normally required only three months credit and were not in direct competition with Cramond. They therefore seem to have been given a reduction of between three and five per cent on their purchases. As the others required six months' credit and com-peted with Cramond they therefore paid accordingly.

The American War of Independence severely curtailed a good market for nails and Cramond had therefore to place its nails wherever it was exporting other items. The company's outlets generally, though not perhaps very large, were widespread ranging as far afield as India and Southern Europe. Curiously enough the nails upon which Cramond prided itself were much less well received than its other products. Constant, Albertini & Co. of Cadiz were interested in hoops for local use, and at first also in nails. They wrote in August 1783 in their rather eccentric French: 'Les Cloux del Etrenger sont defendues pr l'Amerique cependant Il y as moyen de les faire passer. Il n'est pas necessaire d'vous dire que le consumation de cet Article est grande si la qualité en est gouté ce pourquoy le plustôt qu'vous nous passerez ces Enchentillons mieu. . . .' (Foreign nails are forbidden for America, though there are ways of getting them through. Needless to say the consumption of this product is great if the quality of it gives satis-faction. So the sooner you send samples the better.) On 18 November, however, they remark that they have had to give away the nails as a bonus with the hoops because they are 'de peu de valeur et . . . l'on en fait içi à beaucoup melleur marché que chez vous' (of little value . . . and much cheaper ones are made here than with you). At Leghorn there was an import levy on nails, although hoops, files (3000 in one consignment on one occasion), and pottery which the Cadells also made, were readily accepted. The pottery was made at Prestonpans.

There was trouble too with Henry Cort at Gosport. He appeared to have been involved in supplies for the navy, and was interested in obtaining both coal and nails from the Cadells. The relationship was not a happy one. Cramond seemed to have been unable to get Cort's orders right. They were regularly late and also frequently of bad quality. Cort's clerk wrote in January 1779, 'Flatts are used for Oak (& generally Dry Oak) which requires nails to be strait & well made or cannot be drove . . . Mr Cort has already put himself to great inconvenience to get off your nails in general . . . not being able to send one cask without emptying and mixing with a better quality.' The company did not appear to have been entirely to blame for this particular dispute but the variable quality of the nails was a recurring theme in the company's correspondence. In general Cramond depended on regular local sales for its nails. In the week beginning 10 October 1774, for example, nails were despatched to Edinburgh, Duns, Leith (three times), and to Barnbougle for the Earl of Rosebery, and in 1778 the company supplied the nails for building Cramond School.

Half the rod iron made, however, was sold as such, mostly in sizeable consignments to Glasgow, Edinburgh or London, for making nails or 'spike iron'. It was made in a variety of sizes whose measurements were advertised by the company. It was sold in bundles of half a hundredweight, but it was this business of bundling which often caused trouble. Edington, writing to Carron in September 1769 said, '. . . the Iron is carried to the shore in Wheel Barrows & tossed out upon the Beach, afterwards carried in a small Boat to the Sloop . . . it is not therefore no wonder that when the Iron comes to Carron it not only looks ill packed up but is also deficient in Weight.' Bundling always caused trouble and after this instance was used as a reason for providing a small sloop for the company which would be able to come right up to the lowest mill.

A typical order (1761) was for '20 cwt of No. 1, 5 cwt of No. 4, bundles of No. 3 rod', while in 1769 another order called for 12 tons each of No. 1, No. 2, and No. 3, 2 tons of No. 5 and 1 ton each of Nos 8 and 20 rod. In the same year Cramond was told to supply Messrs Cunningham and Co. of Glasgow with 100 tons of No. 1 at the rate of 2 tons a week. Undoubtedly No. 1 and No. 2 rod iron were in greatest demand and the manager was warned in March 1767 to prepare a stock against prospective summer demands comprising 30 tons each of Nos 1 and 2, 10 tons of larger rod iron, and 20 tons of hoop. 'It is best liked when the rods are long drawn, tough iron and carefully tyed', he was told. Complaints were frequently made that the smaller sizes were not made thin enough. Throughout the history of Cramond iron works the slitters were reminded of the need to produce more of the thinner sizes than of the others. During the eighteenth century prices remained fairly stable. In the 1760s it sold at £19 10s or £20 a ton: in 1791 it sold for £18 10s a ton for ready money and presumably slightly more when credit was required.

The next most important product at Cramond was hoops of which up to 18 tons were made weekly. These were used largely by coopers. They were an important item of export to winegrowing areas, especially Spain, Portugal and Madeira and to the West Indies for rum and sugar. The bulk of them were actually sold in London where from 1778 William Hood was the company's agent. Latterly he became a partner but his first dealings with Cramond left him as mystified as us to-day by the variety of technical terms employed. He wrote on 30 April, 'I should like always to have a little remark upon such terms, as you know my present ignorance makes me construe trifles into difficulties . . . a state of ignorance is very disagreeable.' This elicited from Edington a long and detailed list of hoop and rod iron sizes (see Appendix 10), which gives a very clear picture of what Cramond produced. Hood was asked to develop the hoop business as much as possible and Edington wrote to him on 28 May 1778, 'It may be as well to be on good terms with the Ironmongers & to procure orders by giving such a *present* as you may think proper to Mc Culloch's principall Cooper or any other Considerable Cooper taking care that it does not *appear on paper.*'

Other products of importance manufactured at Cramond were spades and shovels, forgings such as files, plough socs and girdles, along with such things as panhandles (often made on order from Carron) and sad iron handles which could be made with the same tools as were used for nail making. Cramond's reputation for its spades survived all changes of management. The company won a prize at the Highland and Agricultural Society's show as late as 1850 for 'both descriptions of draining tools'. The oversight of the spade making in 1795 was the responsibility of Mr Steel with Richard Squair as his craftsman. In that year production reached a thousand dozen. Prices in 1800 were 28s to 34s a dozen for common spades according to size, 33s to 43s for fine spades, 31s to 41s for shovels, and 34s for stable shovels. Spades were manufactured by taking a sheet of iron cut to a length of about $7 \times 4 \times \frac{1}{8}$ inches. Sheets of this size were then linked together by means of scrap steel and beaten out each to a length of $13 \times 7 \times 1/12$ inches. They were then taken to the forge where they were cut, filed and beaten cold. The handles were of hardwood and the blades were straight across the cutting edge.[11]

Files and other small goods were regularly exported from Cramond to America (Virginia) when this was possible, to Genoa and southern Europe and to India via the East India Company. They were also of course sold to Leith. Pan-plate was also manufactured at Cramond mainly for the salt pans of the Forth estuary, especially for Kirkcaldy, which through the nail trade had had close links with Carron from the earliest days. Cramond made different sizes of plate in two standard widths of $10\frac{1}{2}$ or 12 inches and of 19, 20, 21 or 24 inches length.

Although steel was never an important product at Cramond, the company had the distinction of being the first to make steel commercially in Scotland.[12] Iron bars of good quality (usually Swedish, though sometimes Old Sable Russian) were heated in a charcoal furnace for twelve days to increase the carbon content. The resulting metal was known as blister steel and was used for cheap goods. For better quality metal, the blister steel was broken up, bound with faggots, and alternately heated and hammered, resulting in what was known as shear steel. Benjamin Huntsman's crucible steel, by far the best for edge tools and a great advance on anything previously made, was first produced in 1740, but the technique of making it was only slowly accepted. Cramond was still making steel by the old methods in the 1790s. There is not much record of prices: blister steel sold for £28 per ton in 1778, £30 in July 1796, and £32 in November of the same year. By 1812 it was up to £52. Shear steel cost £34 per ton in July 1796 and £36 in November.

IRON AND COAL SUPPLIES

There were four main sources of supply for the iron used at Cramond: Russia, Sweden, Holland and latterly Great Britain, both Scotland and South Wales. Cramond never smelted its own iron: it always imported iron as bar iron (iron after the first stage of refinement had taken place). Up to the mid-eighteenth century most of the bar iron imported into Scotland came from Sweden, but about 1760 Russian iron masters finally came to terms with their serfs and production there rapidly increased. From the 1770s Russia was exporting iron on a very large scale and it became by far the largest source of supply for the Cramond works until the early years of the nineteenth century. Much of the partners' time was taken up during the winter in negotiations with importers and their agents for the next season's supply of iron.

The usual practice seems to have been for the Russian government to allow a certain fixed part of the country's iron produce to be exported each year. This quantity varied considerably. In 1776, 2,107,000 puds or nearly 34,000 tons of iron (1 pud=36 lbs) were available for export from St Petersburg, but in 1775 there seems to have been more, 2,484,000 puds or just over 39,500 tons. This meant that prices tended to fluctuate. In years of scarcity some iron masters held back their iron till the price rose. Iron seems to have been sold to export agents in St Petersburg by auction, so that increasing demand abroad and a limited supply at home tended to the advantage of the Russians.

Within Russia, the iron came mostly from the Urals, and from the large iron ore deposits south of Moscow in the region of Tula and Bryansk. It was also obtained from Olonets in southern Karelia not far from Lake Ladoga and in the form of scrap iron from the Russian Admiralty at St Petersburg.

Early in January each year the company began negotiating with an agent for its iron. Usually the agent was based in London with a correspondent in St Petersburg. Latterly the company also dealt with importers in Leith. In January 1776, for example, Edington closed with Alexander Sutherland, a London agent, for a flat rate of £10 10s per ton for 100 tons of New Sable iron shipped at St Petersburg with the firm option of a further 150 tons at the same price. This was a stroke of good fortune as prices went up shortly afterwards. Sutherland actually sold the iron to Cramond at a loss to himself and did not hesitate to point this out to the company when he tried to solicit their custom again for the following year. That year prices went up and Cramond banded together with John Gillies of Dalnottar and William Robertson of the Smithfield company to buy as much as a thousand tons of iron. Despite Sutherland's advances they went to Hugh Atkins, another London agent, who was prepared to take their order at a flat rate, a method which Cramond always requested but which Sutherland was not prepared to grant a second time. Having reached Britain, the iron was shipped to Leith. Sometimes it came to Leith direct. One minor irritation was that Cramond was not a port in its own right and could not therefore accept foreign merchandise without obtaining the services of a customs officer from Leith. In October 1777, William Cadell tried unsuccessfully to have Cramond recognised as a port. A customs officer was actually resident in Cramond in 1785 and 1792. Cramond never dealt directly with the Russian iron masters though Robertson on one occasion remarked that it might be possible to come to some arrangement with them 'when Mr de Demidoff arrives in England'.

Agents would list the iron they had available in the same way as a vintner listed his wines. Regional disposition came first: Old Sable, New Sable, Brinsko (Bryansk), Tula, Olonitz (Olonets), and Government (these were government run mines mostly in the Urals). Apart from the Government mines, the iron in the Urals was divided into Old and New Sable. Cramond always seemed to have considered Old Sable more valuable; it was certainly more expensive. The name derived from the practice of the iron workers on the Tagil River of stamping a sable on the bars of iron they produced. When those on the Chusovaya River began to do the same their iron became known as New Sable to distinguish it from that made at the older mines.[13] Under these general headings, particular mines were referred to by the names of their owners, or, in the case of the Government mines, by the names of their overseers.[14] Many of the names are those of members of the nobility, the Demidov family in particular being prominent in this field. Others are military men, such as General Chlebnikov who had been rewarded for his services by the gift of iron mines. Others like Turchaninov, Count Worontsov and Major Guriev from the last of whom Cramond frequently purchased iron, had been favourites of the Tsarina Elisabeth. Exceptionally there was such a man as Twerdishev, born a peasant carpenter, who rose to the management of a Government mine. His was the only mine where no serf labour was used and it is of interest in passing that his was one of the very few Russian mines from whose iron Cramond occasionally made steel. There were recognised variations in the quality of the iron from the different mines. The agents often tried to get the manufacturers to buy slightly cheaper iron because it was readily available and would give them (the agents) a better profit. A typical comment from one London agent, with reference to Prince Galitzin's iron read, '. . . tho' 'tis a very pretty Iron, I dare not send it without your permission . . . brittle in its nature but good for nails'. In the 1760s it was actually a good deal more expensive to buy iron from an agent than to get it casually as required, say from an importer in Leith. Even as much as £1 per ton could be saved, but the manufacturers required an absolutely regular supply.

Cramond continued to import Russian iron till at least 1814. After 1804, however, it appears to have been sold as a raw material and not processed at the mills. From 1796 it had risen very sharply in price, partly because of increased export and other taxes in Russia.[15] When the demand for bar iron exceeded what the Russians could supply especially as America was also buying iron, British iron masters were compelled to look elsewhere. Russia had pushed her export of bar iron up to about 49,000 tons in 1793 from 40,000 in 1775. By 1804 one pud of iron delivered at St Petersburg cost only 60 kopeks or approximately 1s 6d, but the mine owners charged around 180 kopeks. In that year the supply dropped quite suddenly by four-fifths. This has been explained by greater internal consumption but the greed of the owners in holding their iron in the hope of a rise in price may also have had something to do with it. Thereafter Cramond along with other Scottish companies seems to have used very little Russian iron.

A second source of supply was Sweden. Swedish iron was of better quality than Russian, but in 1775 was appreciably more expensive at £12 2s 6d per ton at embarkation compared with £10 or slightly more for Russian iron. At Cramond it was used exclusively for making steel. By the mid 1780s the price was down to around £10 per ton while Russian was about £12 12s though there were stiff handling charges of various sorts to be paid which cancelled out the difference. Cramond never seemed to have taken more than 50 tons of Swedish iron in any one year, partly from Gothenburg and partly from Öregrund near Stockholm. Another source of supply came from Amsterdam and Middleburg in the Low Countries. Collection of scrap metal was a profitable trade in the Netherlands as in this country. The import of this scrap along with the use of the enormous quantity of old nuts, bolts, rivets, axes, shovels and plate metal available at any large seaport constituted a useful source of raw material.

Finally there was the home supply. The rising prices of foreign pig iron had induced manufacturers to try to produce it themselves. Carron had smelted iron ore from the first, but Cramond through the activities of Edington was one of the first iron mills to extend its activities to the working of locally mined and smelted iron ore. Edington who had long been chafing in the rather confined atmosphere of Cramond set up the Clyde Iron Works along with John McKenzie of Strathgarve in December 1786, and on 7 April following William Cadell or, if he chose, one of his sons, was admitted to the partnership. Production was under way in 1788, when the new company supplied Cramond with a set of rollers. Clyde was not particularly successful. William Cadell wrote in May 1811, 'We have had our Rubs in Life, & that at Clyde entered into with the advice of Friends has indeed been a bad one. . . .' It was almost immediately followed by the foundation of the works at Muirkirk in Lanarkshire where both coal and ironstone were to be found in close proximity. Several works operating on the same lines as Cramond had an interest in it. John Gillies of Dalnottar and William Robertson of the Smithfield Company were both partners. The effect of these operations was to raise the production of bar iron in Scotland from about 1500 tons in 1788, to about 16,000 tons in 1796. In July 1796, Cramond empowered Edington to treat with Muirkirk for a regular supply of bar iron, 5 to 10 tons weekly, and by October, Muirkirk was definitely to supply 5 or 6 tons a week up to the following May. In addition Mather of Duffield, near Derby, was to provide 30 or 40 tons by March.

The stock of bar iron at Cramond in November 1796 was listed as follows: 218 tons of Swedish and Old Sable iron destined for hoops, steel and plate; 146 tons of New Sable and 138 tons of British iron, 60 from England (Duffield), 28 from Muirkirk, and 50 from Carron, all destined for rod iron, the Scottish iron being used for the smaller rods. The proportions were about the same in 1799 but thereafter the proportion of British iron rose steadily. It is difficult to be sure exactly how much bar iron was used in any one year. 420 tons seem to have been used in 1766, 710 in 1778, and 650 in 1794. These are minimum figures and may well have been eked out by purchases from Leith importers or from Carron as occasion required. On the other hand William Cadell always saw himself as a merchant dealing in bar iron and it could be that not all the bar iron at Cramond at any one time was actually to be used there.

The other large item of raw material that the company had to find was coal. The exact accounts for this period have not survived but, from March 1766 to March 1767, the company hoped to use only 250 tons of coal at 8s a ton for 500 tons of finished goods, rising possibly to 400 tons for 800 tons of finished goods. In 1768, however, the average expenditure on coal was actually £21 10s per month, giving an approximate annual consumption of 645 tons in the production of probably a smaller weight in finished goods. Complaints were made by the Carron management in 1762 that too much coal was being used and that ideally half a ton of coal should produce half a ton of finished work, i.e. that 4s worth of coal should do what was currently requiring 10s worth. It was further reckoned that the works should be able to do 12 or 14 heats, slitting 6 or 7 cwts each, in every 24 hours. This gave a theoretical production of 20 tons a week, compared with 24 at a slitting mill near Birmingham and with the 12 tons a week that Cramond usually turned out. In fact Cramond always exceeded its theoretical coal requirements. In the projected consumption given above, it was expected that the works would produce 500 tons of finished iron. If the consumption of 1768 is typical the company had not much improved its efficiency in the matter of coal from the figures of 1762. The main problem, discussed below, was the frequent reheatings which were required and in 1762 the company recommended to the manager at Cramond that the furnaces should be filled over the weekend with 'culm and ashes' so as to keep them warm. After 1770 when all coal used seems to have come from the Grange colliery there are no figures for consumption except that, between March and May 1775, Grange despatched 102 tons for Cramond.

THE MILL MACHINERY

In 1750 the work consisted of the two lowest mills, only one of which, Cockle Mill, was in use for the iron trade. Fairafar was not developed as a forge until after 1770, although it was bought by the Smith and

Wright Work Company to ensure a good flow of water at the lower mill. Cockle Mill had only two furnaces, although in 1767 it had been suggested that a third should be added. Power for the slitting and rolling machinery was produced exclusively by water. When Cockle Mill was a corn mill, a much smaller dam, still partly visible, had been used, which ran straight across the river at its narrowest point, about 25 yards below the east end of the present dam. The Smith and Wright Work Company received permission from Sir John Inglis to make a new dam which they did in 1751. It was of masonry lined with wood and occupied the position of the present dam. It was sufficiently substantial to be used as a footbridge across the river.

When John Rennie the great engineer, and later the designer of the new Cramond Bridge, visited the works as a young man in 1782, he wrote a description of the mill machinery which gives a clear idea of how it operated. There seem to have been three wheels at Cockle Mill, each about 16 feet in diameter and 5 feet broad, two for slitting and one for rolling, and one at Fairafar for the forge. A Swedish visitor to the mills in 1802 observed that all the wheels were undershot although some of them were technically breast wheels. He also observed that the canopy over the forge which saved a great deal of coal, was in constant need of repair, and that the framework of the forge was almost entirely of iron, very little timber having been used. Even the haft of the forge hammer was in that material. Rennie was struck by the same thing and noted that much of the machinery was in metal including some of the wheels and axles. This was an extremely up to date arrangement and was probably attributable to the influence of John Smeaton who had been called in to improve the machinery at Carron. In a letter of January 1766, Samuel Garbett wrote to William Cadell, 'The manner of putting water upon the wheels at Cramond and the form of them is a matter of such consequence as requires great consideration, and I think Mr Smeaton's and Brindley's opinion should be taken. . . . I shall see Brindley in London the latter end of this month.' It has always been said that the first mill to make use of iron in its machinery was Rennie's Albion Mills in London, begun in 1784, and the fact that Rennie mentions iron several times in his account shows that it was of great interest. The machinery at Cramond was, however, in constant need of repair. The new rollers supplied in October 1760 were ruined by 1765. The wheels were also in bad condition and Edington had to have them repaired for the summer of

1766. For this sort of work the services of William Gowans from Drumsheugh were engaged. When actual pieces of machinery were required they were obtained from Carron or later from Clyde Iron Works. Repairs to the dams were done by local labour using stone from quarries on the Cramond estate.

SPACE AND MONEY PROBLEMS

The lower valley of the Almond, though suitable for milling on a small scale, was not well adapted for several reasons to large industrial undertakings. In November 1765, Edington wrote to Carron, 'The fall of water here is very little, by that we are probably obliged to heat the iron more than they do in England, as it is long in going through the Rollers and Cutters & consequently must be a great deal colder than when the wheels go with Double Velocity.' Despite periodic improvements to the water wheels, lack of power remained a problem right up to the introduction of a steam engine in 1854. It obliged the company to use more coal than its rivals and it also produced more waste iron. William Cadell calculated that in 1765, out of 400 tons of iron manufactured into rods and hoops over 24¾ tons were wasted as compared with an equivalent loss of 14 tons in Staffordshire. This loss was reckoned to be worth £162.

Perhaps the greatest single disadvantage in the lower valley was the tide which could flood the wheel at Cockle Mill to a depth of nine feet at high tide and so stop work at the mill for several hours in one day.

Space was also a problem in the confined valley. Even at Cockle Mill where some expansion might have taken place, the company was limited by the need to lease its land from the Inglis family. As both the Inglis and Rosebery families were interested in improving their estates they did not care for the presence of the industry, let alone its expansion, on their very doorsteps. They both tried (Inglis in 1775, Rosebery in 1787) to frustrate the company's activities in the Courts.

The works also suffered from the economic depression which afflicted Scotland from the summer of 1772 until the end of the century. The failure of the Ayr Bank in June, followed by that of at least ten private banks in Edinburgh, meant that credit was difficult to obtain. In a business such as that at Cramond where capital investment was large but returns were slow, this was particularly unfortunate. The American War of Independence also made difficulties by cutting off a good market and a source of raw material. As early as 1773, William Cadell was using his influence with Thomas Dundas to prevent a certain Edward Quincey from starting a slitting mill in New England. Cadell was only too aware that the value of the works and trade as stated in the company's books considerably exceeded their actual market value at that time. He still had confidence in the business. In a memorandum to Edington dated 12 November 1774, he remarked, 'As to the price of the Mill & value of the Trade we are not willing to have them considered as less than they stand in the Books . . . because prior to the stagnation of sales in July 1772 it was one of the most Profitable Trades in this Country . . . and may be so again when the sales revive.'

The Cramond Works seemed to have flourished during the eighteenth century by avoiding unnecessary expense and capital outlay

Valuation	Valuation less share capital	Valuation	Valuation less share capital
1778 £13286:5:10	£4286:5:10	1788 £23418:12:1	£15218:12:1
1779 £12436:10:11	£4436:10:11	1789 £24144:8:5	£15944:8:5
1780 £10858:10:9	£2625:10:9	1790 £24282:9:5	£16082:9:5
1781 £12005:6:9	£3805:6:9	1791 £27949:14:1½	£19749:14:1½
1782 £14217:19:9	£6017:19:9	1792 £30148:16:7½	£21948:16:7½
1783 £16920:-:10	£8720:-:10	1793 £31124:9:10½	£22924:9:10½
1784 £17150:10:5½	£8950:10:5½	1794 £32785:19:1½	£24585:19:1½
1785 £17594:-:5	£9394:-:5	1795 £34287:5:3	£26087:5:3
1786 £19621:19:-	£11421:19:-	1796 £25527:3:1	£25527:3:1
1787 £21336:6:7	£13136:6:7		

1778 includes £9000 share capital, 1779 £8000, 1780 to 1795 £8000 plus £200 interest. The figure for 1796 includes no share capital which explains the apparent sudden drop of nearly £10,000 from the previous year.

and confining activities to the small number of products for which it had gained some reputation. The finances of the Company in the eighteenth century are not easy to ascertain as the actual accounts have not survived. We do, however, have the overall annual valuation of

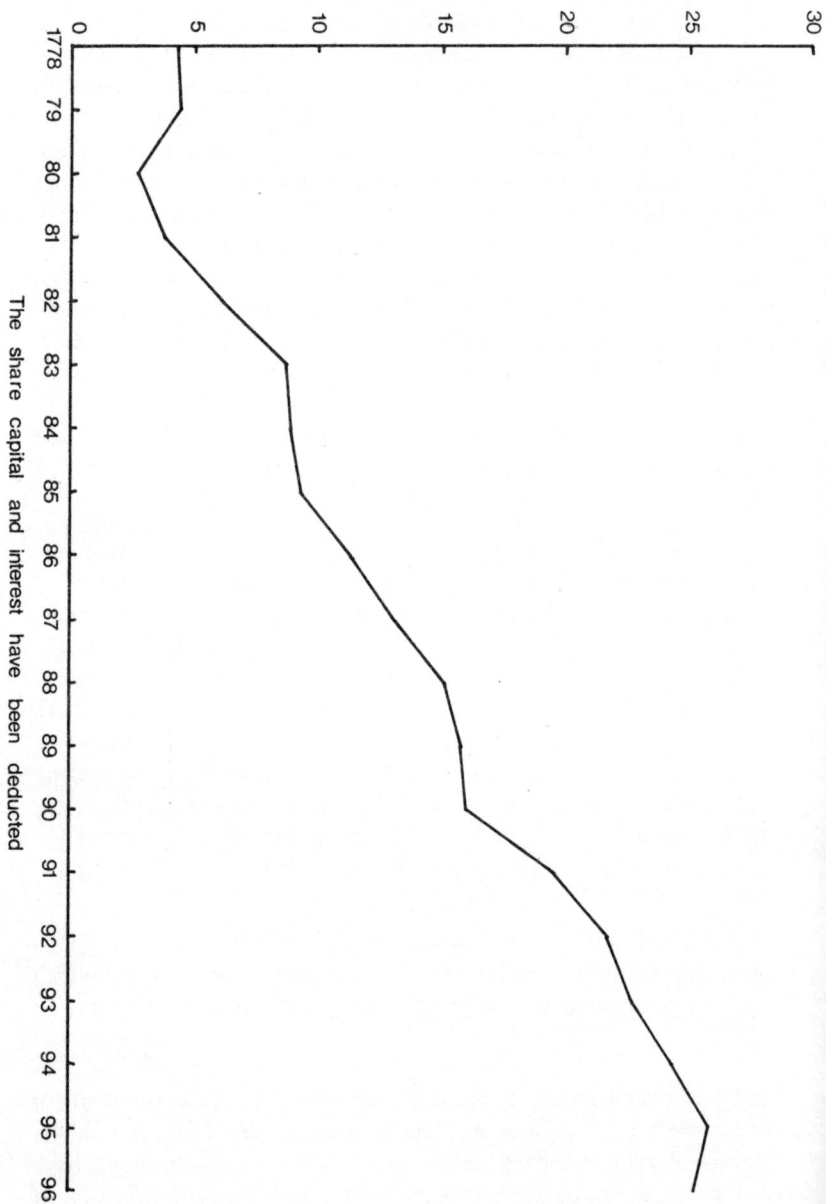

Annual valuation (in £000s)

The share capital and interest have been deducted

24

Plate 3 *Fairafar Mill* engraved by James Stewart in about 1840
The large undershot wheel on the south wall of the building can be seen, with
a rim-drive subsidiary wheel above. Cinder and slag is being dumped in the
river where it may still be found. In the background is Cockle Mill
By courtesy of Edinburgh Public Libraries

Plate 4 *Peggie's Mill* taken in 1966
The main lade can clearly be seen on the right flowing to the
main water-wheel beyond a protective grill. On the left is a
small subsidiary overshot wheel
By courtesy of *The Scotsman*

Plate 5 *Dowie's Mill Cottages* taken in 1895
A view of typical mill-workers' housing
By courtesy of Edinburgh Public Libraries

the various businesses of the Cadell family. The figure opposite shows the value of the moveables and the business of the Cramond Iron Works on 1 January of each year from 1778 to 1796 taken from the abstract of the valuation.

THE NEW GENERATION

It is clear that the company prospered until about 1797. The share capital of £8000 was made up of 16 shares divided among William and John Cadell and Thomas Edington. William was the senior partner and presumably had a greater share than the others but it is not clear how the shares were actually allocated. These arrangements were altered in the 1790s when the families of all the partners were growing up. In December 1794 John Cadell asked whether he could hand over his share (2/16) to his eldest son William (1773-1840), later treasurer of the Bank of Scotland. This was agreed as William was well known, having already been employed by the company as an overseer from 1790. The two other partners were empowered to hand over their shares to their eldest sons when they came of age. In August 1795 there was a number of changes. William Hood who had been the company's London agent for 18 years became a partner and the shares, now 28, were divided ten to William Cadell sen., three to John Cadell, three to William Cadell jun., four to Hood and eight to Edington. From this time on the younger members of the senior William's family began to take an active interest in the firm, first as employees and then as partners. George Cadell (1777-1806) was employed from 1797, Alexander (1781-1821) from 1800, Philip (1782-1854) from 1808. Alexander who spent most of his active life as a civil servant in Ceylon seemed to have had a share in Cramond. His share may have passed on his death to James John (1779-1858) who was for a time employed at Clyde. William Archibald (1775-1855), the eldest son, may at one time have had a share in Cramond. He certainly put up money for it but he never took an active part in its affairs. The younger William Cadell's association with the company seems to have come to an end about 1800. Alexander may perhaps have taken over his share. Philip probably took on that of George but that is merely conjecture. The Edington family seems to have slipped out of the business altogether about 1800, probably with some relief, since Edington had been trying to broaden his activities since 1777.

The only set of production cost figures which have survived from this period are those for 1766. Exclusive of the price of the raw materials, it was reckoned that the manufacture of 100 tons of hoops and 300 tons of rod iron cost £565 7s, of which £315 was for rod iron, and £250 for hoops. The 420 tons of bar iron required for the manufacture cost £14 15s a ton on delivery, a total of £6195. With an additional £120 for general purposes (William Cadell seems to have included this figure twice) there is an outlay of £6880 7s against a revenue of £7800: £5700 for the rod iron at £19 a ton, and £2100 for the hoops at £21 a ton, giving a credit balance of £920. This was respectable in a small firm with a small staff, but in 1811, the only other year before the mid-nineteenth century for which any sort of figure has survived, the credit for rod iron was only just over £800, half of what was thought proper.

By the end of the first decade of the nineteenth century Cramond was no longer of any importance as an iron works. This was principally because the works were too small in area and in capital. With the cheapening of British bar iron larger and wealthier firms could expand in a way that Cramond could not. Cramond did not have the ability to profit from new techniques. While admitting frequently that with the greater expense of producing iron goods there it was essential to concentrate on high quality products, it equally frequently failed to do so. The company never really recovered from the financial crisis of 1797, which had shaken the Cadell family finances severely. The only reason for clinging to Cramond until 1860 was that it was not possible to sell it, or at least not at a price that seemed reasonable.

From 1808 the management of the firm seems almost exclusively to have been in the hands of Philip Cadell, the younger son of William Cadell sen. He was, according to Marjory Fleming, a man of great charm and of great if momentary enthusiasms.[16] Unfortunately he suffered from depressions which could prevent his doing anything for days on end, when he usually retired to his bed. On at least two occasions his father had to send someone to get him up. In a letter to his brother, James John, in January 1815 he described himself well, 'I am a man of keen feelings and much easier hurt than you seem to have had any idea of, my disposition is also very determined and cannot bear contradiction in any of my plans, and when I conceive this is done

I don't care what expence I am put to in bringing my object round.' Philip had an illegitimate son, another Philip, who went to California at the time of the gold rush, and tried to establish an outlet for Cramond spades there.

Philip had started his career at the family paper works at Auchendinny. He was in fact more interested in paper, and more knowledgeable about it than he ever was about iron. He took over a firm which was not doing well, and he realised quite rightly that modernisation was urgent, requiring a large amount of money to be spent. Unfortunately the money was not readily available. To raise it he had to obtain loans on the security of the buildings at Cramond. Besides he was not the right kind of man to carry through a large project of the kind. In his father's phrase he was inclined to 'suffer from being too sanguine'. In 1809, Philip thought of selling Cramond and buying land instead but this seems to have come to nothing. What he did accomplish was to start a paper mill at Peggie's Mill. With the end of the Napoleonic wars the demand for iron diminished. It was therefore wise to try to diversify the work at Cramond by the introduction of a new product. Unfortunately the water turned out to be unsuitable for the production of any but the coarsest paper, a type of cartridge paper used only in the hosiery industry. In fact the papermaking activities at Cramond never showed more than a very modest profit. Philip was nevertheless optimistic. In October 1815 he wrote, 'I fear it would be a difficult matter to get rid of the Cramond concern in these times, but if we had 2 or 3 vats at work at P'mill I think it would ease the Cramond Iron trade and bring in 5 or £600 a year but with little increase of capital.'

Philip's financial rashness put Cramond in a difficult position. If it had been possible, the whole concern would have been sold. This had been mooted as early as 1797 but had never taken place because the company had never had a good enough offer. In December 1826 William Archibald wrote to James John, 'One obvious cause of your unpleasant circumstances is your having rejected Lord Rosebery's offer for Cramond and afterwards Mr Laurie's. I do not know how you can justify the refusal of such advantageous offers in the situation in which you are.' William Archibald's concern was partly due to what he considered the misappropriation of £10,000 which had come back to the family on the death of Alexander Cadell in 1821. It seems to have been put into Cramond but no satisfactory explanation ever seems to have been given as to how it was used.

From about 1815 the family records relating to Cramond become fragmentary. This may be an accident of history or it may have been an act of policy to destroy the evidence of a period of no great credit. The fact is that there is virtually no information about Cramond until 1847, the year in which the company was refounded on new lines.

Two maps of the mills at Cramond have survived, one made by J. Ainslie about 1787 and another by Thomas Carfrae in 1839. While little evidence survives in the Cadell papers for changes which took place during these years, the two maps clearly indicate a number of developments. By 1839, the old dam at Fairafar had been superseded by the waterfall opposite the mill as it is today, some hundred yards further downstream. A small tramway had also been constructed between Fairafar Mill and the mooring at Cockle Mill. A branch of this appears to have run up the School Brae. The buildings at Cockle Mill were also greatly extended before 1839. The range of office buildings had been considerably lengthened and Cadell's Row had been built.

CHAPTER 3

THE FINAL PHASE OF THE MILLS

The Cramond Company was refounded in 1847 with new articles of copartnery and a new and more solid financial basis. Philip Cadell who had continued to manage the company despite increasing incompetence went bankrupt in 1845 and was forced to give up his management at Cramond. He retired to Trinity, Edinburgh, and then to Stirling where he died in 1854. The new partnership was to take on the debts and liabilities of the 'Old Company' as they stood in the company's books on 30 June 1846. It was deemed to have started at that date but the articles to copartnery were not finally agreed upon until 9 May 1848. This delay was caused, partly at least, by James John's alarm at the prospect of being very largely responsible himself as landowner and chief partner for any debts that might be incurred. It was therefore decided that he should have an annual rent of £700 plus £50 for 'the Erections at Dowie's Mill and the Steel Tilt at the Cockle Mill', and that the shares should be divided equally—£2000 to each of the five partners—instead of making James John the largest shareholder as had originally been proposed. The estimated value of the works in 1846 was £21,070.

The original partners of the new company were James John as landowner; William, James John's eldest son (1810-1862) who had been a partner for about ten years; Henry (1812-1888), James John's second son, by far the ablest member of the family, who was never a resident partner. (He had just taken on at that time the management of the Duke of Buccleuch's coal mines at Dalkeith. He was, however, always consulted if there was any matter in dispute.) George Philip (1820-1896), the youngest son of James John, who at that time was principal clerk at the Grange colliery, having abandoned a naval career as the result of an accident. William Phipps who had been employed at Cramond as early as 1808 and had become a partner by 1836, having been principal book-keeper for ten years or so. Phipps was a nephew of J. P. Wood and was therefore distantly connected to the Cadells, since Wood had married Marion Cadell, a cousin of James John. The partnership was to continue for twelve years unless dissolved earlier, and Phipps and William were to continue as resident managers.

Phipps died in January 1851 and the company managed to prevent his son, Thomas, from taking his place. He was succeeded by Alexander Cadell (1818-1860), another son of James John, who had been employed by the company before 1838 when, thinking he was learning little, he left and made two voyages to the West Indies. He then returned 'soured with the sea' in Henry's phrase, and settled at Grange. About 1848 he moved to Cramond and became a partner in 1851. He married, at Demerara, Agnes Delaforce who died in the very early morning of 1 January 1851 while returning to Cramond from the papermakers' ball at Peggie's Mill. She fell into the river, and her body was eventually washed up at Bervie, north of Montrose.

The only other persons of importance employed at Cramond during this period were Lawrence Dow who worked as a traveller from about 1841 and latterly as a bookkeeper in moments of emergency but who was dismissed for dishonesty in October 1854, and William Bennet who came from Valleyfield as a boy in September 1851 to help in the office. Bennet turned out to be a very able clerk but it is interesting to see how his ability was resented by William and Alexander and how he almost automatically formed an alliance with Henry. He married a daughter of Thomas Aird, the tenant of the sawmill at Dowie's Mill.

James John was nervous about the situation and very doubtful of the abilities of the managers. He wrote to Henry in December 1847, '. . . it is quite disgusting to see the indifference & ignorance both of Mr Phipps and Willm as to almost everything about the work.' It was now thought advisable to engage a manager strictly for the machinery and Robert Orr, previously of the Ayrshire Iron Company, was engaged early in 1848 for £120 per annum and a free house.

This reflected a preoccupation with technology which continued till the final demise of the company in 1860. By 1847, the Cramond Iron Works had become very old fashioned, being small, and powered, even in the heyday of the steam engine, exclusively by water. Apart from giving less power than steam and being subject to fluctuations according to the state of the river, water gave a rather uneven force, the result of which was that the machinery was frequently jolted with consequent breakages of gear wheels and even of the water wheels themselves. The references to broken-down machinery in the early years of the new company are very frequent.

The tilt hammer was being repaired in December 1847 and a new boiler and new pinions were being fitted in the mill work at Peggie's Mill. The wheel at Cockle Mill was under repair in September 1848. Stoppages of this kind were causing serious loss as James John wrote in January 1849, '£50 a week loss would frighten anybody'. Orr left the company in the summer of 1849, as he felt it did not have enough work to keep him occupied. The mechanical difficulties went on. The wheel driving the new tilt was giving trouble in June 1850 and a millwright, named Brown, who was examining the machinery, was crushed to death between the wheel and the breast when the forgeman turned on the water without knowing he was there. The following February the large spurwheel at Cockle Mill broke. It was 13 feet in diameter and 12¾ inches broad. A spurwheel is the first wheel in a mill-train following the water-wheel or the steam-engine. It had only been installed five years before but was reckoned the weakest wheel in the whole mill. Some of the oak teeth which were a good deal worn had broken and had been replaced. Ten days later they broke again and the whole wheel collapsed. This was an opportunity to replace a wooden wheel with an iron one. William suggested that the iron wheel could well be smaller and that by increasing the size of the next wheel in the train which was only about 3 feet 3 inches in diameter the mill could be kept working at the same speed. It is not clear how this repair was carried out. There was further complaint of broken pinions in September 1851.

The first mention of a steam engine occurs on 28 June 1852 when Alexander apparently had a plan for introducing one. It is not clear what it was to do. It may have been the same as the engine for the hammer about which he sought advice in February 1853. It was about that time that a small steam engine was introduced to drive lathes, a fan blast, and a vertical drilling and cutting machine. In September 1853, the big water wheel at Cockle Mill gave way. This finally precipitated the change to steam. In October estimates for the installation of a steam engine were sought and in December that of Messrs Yule and Wilkie, of £575, was accepted. By 17 April 1854 part of the engine was already on the way and the engine was finally put into operation in September.

Henry Cadell described this engine in January 1855. 'This engine is 50 horses power (being a high pressure engine, Cylr. 26 inch with 4 feet stroke) when well kept in steam goes easily driving all the machinery. At present there are three boilers 6 feet diameter and 15 feet over the hemispherical ends, wrought from the waste heat of two heating and puddling furnaces.' This completely superseded the water wheel and was found perfectly satisfactory for processing large sizes of iron. For small sizes, however, for which a lot of movement was required it was not sufficiently powerful and an extra boiler was ordered early in 1855. There were other problems to be faced before the situation improved. Yule and Wilkie demanded extra payment for the spurwheel which they had provided along with the engine but Cramond held that it was included in the original estimate. The case went to arbitration and Cramond lost. Then in February 1855 there was such a severe frost that even with fires lit under them the pipes leading to the steam engine froze and the whole mill was put out of action. In mid April the base plate of the whole engine was discovered to be fractured and had to be replaced. After that, things seem to have gone very much better although in 1857 and 1858 there was trouble once more with gear wheels and various parts of the mill train. A new steam hammer was introduced in 1858 and met with some opposition from the Cramond estate. Inglis was prepared to allow it to be used only on one site, between Fairafar and Cockle Mills. This was not altogether satisfactory to the company but it was eventually erected there.

With the introduction of steam Henry considered it theoretically possible to raise the company's output to 3625 tons of finished iron annually. This would have reduced overheads to such an extent that the company might have become reasonably competitive once more. In fact the steam engine only increased production to an average of 1522 tons per year for the years 1855-9 compared with 1013 tons for the years 1846-54. This increase did not even bring in more money as can be seen from the profit and loss figures for those years (see the table on p. 74). There was a slight increase in profits in 1856 and 1857, but the following year they were worse than ever.

The reason for this was partly that the extra machinery that should have been installed with the steam engine, a new set of puddlers' rolls and a pair of shears at Cockle Mill, and a heavy hammer at Fairafar, was not acquired at once. At the same time the price of finished work was going down and only by rapid expansion could the company hope to keep going. In 1854 common iron sold at £10 10s and forgings at £13 10s a ton. In January 1855 prices at Cramond were reduced by 10s per ton all round. In Staffordshire they had gone down by £2. They appear to have been lowered again before 1860. As long as Cramond failed to reduce its production costs there was little hope of its profitability, and news such as the publication of Bessemer's process in 1856 was found very discouraging. There were also hidden financial problems such as unpaid rents and interest due to James John which by 1858 had risen to £14,387. In addition the works themselves seemed to have declined in value from about £21,000 in 1846 to about £10,500 in 1859.

Of the smaller manufactures at Cramond only spades and paper seem to have been reasonably profitable. Paper, although of an inferior quality and made without the machinery which had long been in use elsewhere, generally showed a profit. A new boiler was installed in April 1856. In 1859 the mill equipment at Peggie's Mill consisted of mill buildings with a water fall of ten feet. The buildings included a drying loft with size-house beneath and a further detached loft and washhouse, mill machinery including 2 vats, 3 presses, pipes, etc., a finishing house and rag house, a rag shed and three paper presses. There was a foreman's house and two other dwelling houses with grounds of about 9½ acres.

The production figures for paper have not survived except for the years 1846-51, during which time the quantity of paper made dropped from 71 tons 16 cwts to 42 tons 5 cwts, with a minimum of 20 tons 6 cwts in 1850. The quantity of rags used, however, fell more steeply, from 102 tons in 1846 to 23 tons in 1850. This indicated a great increase in efficiency if not in output.

The spades maintained the high standard set by Squair, winning a prize at the Highland and Agricultural Society's show in 1850. The work was done at Dowie's Mill which also included a sawmill run by Thomas Aird who was succeeded by his son Thomas. The sawmill turned out handles for the spades and also supplied sawdust for some of the forging processes. It operated independently of the iron works and employed six men on its own account. Dowie's Mill consisted in 1859 of a forge and buildings, with a furnace and chimney, two hearth fires, an anvil, two water wheels, blast fanners, etc., a waterfall of 7 feet 10 inches with dam and sluices, an eight-roomed house, four smaller houses of which one was the foreman's and another was occupied by Thomas Aird, a turning shop with a warehouse above, the sawmill with a wooden water wheel, shed and saw bench, a shaftbending or boiler house, old nail and chain shops, foreman's workshop with three hearths, and the spade finishing shop, with five fires and a warehouse

33

above. The mill also included a garden and about 1½ acres of land. A considerable quantity of spades continued to be made up to 1860. Nail work, if it was still done, must have been on a very small scale indeed.

Even with all these mechanical improvements the company still laboured under one great disadvantage and that was a personal one. It was not run by people who were suited to the job. As far back as 1837, Henry Cadell wrote in his diary, 'My father's operations . . . are doing very ill . . . principally (I think) from his injudicious way of managing matters & from his leaving Cramond work to Mr Phipps (a man in my opinion quite incapable of managing a work of the kind) without almost any restraint or controul. He is involving himself in debt & with the prospect of in a short time bringing bankruptcy on himself he will not be in the least advised by his friends to place that restraint upon the management of that work which might make it a profitable concern instead of a swamp for money.' Phipps certainly was not up to this responsibility. He had been a competent bookkeeper but his abilities as a manager had always been suspect. Latterly his honesty had been called in question when he drew double his annual salary from the company's funds in the year before he died.

William Cadell was little better. Alexander writing to Henry in 1853, said, 'I have been inclined to complain of Willm's Conduct all winter, but now have to do it, in consequence of the injury he is doing to the works, especially in not answering the correspondence & ordering things wanted, in fact non-attendance through the day. He is also harming Mr Bennet, as he gets him to come up at night to direct the invoices which should be done through the day, where the boy has to stay till 10 or 11 o'clock at night. We have lost several good Customers lately with not having answered letters till they had written 2 or 3 times for an answer, so if dull times come we may count on being at a stand. . . . I will be obliged if you can come over soon as I will not stand so much abuse as he gave me last night before a lot of the men when he was the worse of drink.'

In fact the books were never up to date before the arrival of Bennet. Serious mistakes went undetected for years, and even after his arrival there were frequent delays in making up the quarterly and annual statements because he could not get access to the relevant ledgers. It was not surprising that Bennet who was an able man and went on to a managerial position in an iron works at Gartness near Airdrie found the situation galling. He often complained to Henry. His efficiency aroused instant opposition in the managers who found him a reproach to their idleness.

The original partnership was to last only for twelve years and by 1858 the company was looking for buyers. First of all in March 1859 Alexander tried to buy out the other partners for a total of £10,500. His valuation was contested especially in respect of Peggie's and Dowie's Mills which he valued at £2056 and £1370 respectively compared with Landale & Sons' valuation of £3867 and £1797. Alexander proposed also to rent the lower mills from Inglis for £350 a year on condition that the railway was brought to Cramond (probably along the shore from Granton) as had recently been projected. He died in December 1860 and was followed by William in 1862. Inglis appears to have bought Cockle and Fairafar mills himself in 1861 and Alexander was succeeded in the two upper mills which the family actually owned by James John Cadell (1851-72) only son of William. Peggie's Mill was leased in 1862 by Michael Jack of Horton near Grantham who with his son John employed 38 people at papermaking. Paper production ceased in September 1881. In November 1877, the two upper mills were sold by James John's trustees to John Mackay and the family's connection with Cramond came to an end.

John Mackay was a manufacturing chemist and used Peggie's Mill as a gelatine works probably from 1881 after Jack's departure until about 1922. He also owned Dowie's Mill which he leased as a sawmill from 1871-81 to Henry Parker who was also associated with the Wood-hall Mill, Juniper Green. Next came William Bertram a wood turner and from 1896 John Weller.

Weller was a Newcastle man who specialised in cheap furniture.[17] When about 1916, he decided to emigrate to California he packed up all his machinery and left Dowie's Mill on a lease to Ernest Didcock who with his brothers James and Arthur had come from High Wycombe to work with Weller. Weller found that California did not suit him and came back about 1922. He tried to get Dowie's Mill back from Didcock. When unsuccessful he set up a rival furniture-making business at Peggie's Mill. There was considerable bickering between the two concerns over water in the dry months, mainly because Peggie's Mill depended upon a steady flow of water to drive an electricity generator. When Didcock's lease was up in 1934 Weller resumed possession of Dowie's Mill and the Didcock business moved to Gorgie where it still flourishes. Weller continued his furniture-making at Peggie's Mill until the beginning of the 1939 war when shortage of labour and the need to produce furniture to very limited specifications put him out of business. Under the Didcock family the furniture business had been a large one, employing as many as 30 men, and using for the most part local timber, especially beech which was obtained from Barnton (150 trees were taken from that estate between 1925 and 1934), Clermiston, Carlowrie and Dalmeny. The actual occupier of Dowie's Mill from 1934 was a scrap metal merchant called Tully. The mill wheel unfortunately was completely smashed shortly afterwards, perhaps in the flood which destroyed Fairafar, and its use as a mill probably ceased then.

The lower mills continued to be used for the iron trade for a few years after the departure of the Cadells. By 1862 they were in the hands of The Cramond Iron Works, a new firm about which little seems to be known. They must have had a certain amount of money to invest in the concern, as in April 1867 there was a complaint by John Milne, the parish schoolteacher to the heritors, that the plaster in all the rooms of his house was cracking due to the 'large hammers at the new iron mill'.[18] According to the valuation rolls however, the iron works had disappeared by 1873 and a paintworks owned by the British and Oriental Ship Coating Company had premises at or near Cockle Mill. This concern first appears in the valuation rolls in 1869 and ceases again in 1876. From then it would seem that the buildings were used only occasionally for stabling. By the end of the century the mill was already ruinous. Fairafar was largely demolished by a flood in 1935 although the mill buildings must have been fairly complete up till then. Since then what was once an important industrial centre has become a place for boating and Sunday walks and the industry in the parish has moved eastwards to Granton and to Edinburgh.

CHAPTER 4

THE MILL SITES

Some description must be given of what little remains of this once flourishing industrial settlement in 1972-3.

At Dowie's Mill there are still a row of cottages and the detached Primrose Cottage, situated on the right of the path as you go downstream. This is all that survives of a large group of workers' homes which in 1841, for example, housed a total population of 77 of whom 28 were actually employed at the mills.[19]

The weir at Dowie's Mill is, apart from that at Fairafar, the best preserved of the mill weirs or damheids as they were called. It was extensively repaired and perhaps heightened in 1910. Although there is now a breach twenty feet wide in the middle, it is otherwise in relatively good condition. The weir gave a fall of $7\frac{1}{2}$ feet and supplied water to the mill lead through two sluice gates of which the wooden sockets are still visible. A smaller sluice in the dam itself immediately beside the entrance to the lead allowed excessive water to escape downstream. The lead ran underground on the line of the present path coming into the open beside Primrose Cottage.

The ground level has risen considerably as a result of tipping and demolition work and the undergrowth is particularly luxuriant. It is still possible, however, to determine the point of entry of the wheel shaft into the ruined wall opposite Primrose Cottage, although with fresh dumping actually going on, this will not be possible much longer. This shows the position of the mill shop. The positions of other buildings can be detected in the extremely overgrown waste area between the path and the river. The two small subsidiary leads can be seen returning to the river at right angles to the main lead. One of these, two feet across and about four feet deep, is in reasonable repair for its last 20 feet. The main lead rejoined the river just above the second weir through a sluice 6 feet 6 inches wide and still partly visible. For a list of the buildings and fittings here and at Peggie's Mill, see p. 49.

The second weir now very much decayed, fed water into a large lead

37

which ran a quarter of a mile down the valley along the line of the present path to Peggie's Mill. The entrance to the lead is just visible in the form of a dressed stone slab embedded across the path. At the point where the lead entered the mill buildings enough survives to allow measurements. It appears to have been eleven feet wide and four feet deep.

Peggie's Mill was the last in operation but there is now less of it than of any other. If the public path did not cross the floor of the main mill shop it would be difficult to know where it was as the undergrowth and the loose earth from the adjacent building site threaten to engulf the whole area. The works originally had two large buildings, the foundations of which up to a height of five feet on the river side have survived. Of the workers' cottages up the hillside nothing remains. The main lead emptied into the river just below the mill but a small lead turned off it at right angles. Its entrance sluice survived in 1965 but seems to have been covered up since.

The next weir, just under ten feet high, is the impressive waterfall at Fairafar. Before the reconstruction in 1935, the lead from the weir followed the line of the steps on the footpath and passed under one of the mill buildings to join the river again about 100 yards further north. A branch of it turned left before entering the buildings and drove a wheel mounted on the south wall of the mill. This wheel, from the position of the scrape marks on the wall must have been 13 feet in diameter and this agrees very well with the wheel shown in an engraving of about 1820 by James Stewart entitled *Scene on the River Almond*.[20] Looking at Fairafar from immediately upstream Stewart shows the wheel on the facing wall and another wheel on the river side with a distant view of Cockle Mill. The large arched opening in the mill can be seen through which the shaft of the wheel entered the mill perhaps to operate the great forge hammer. Subsidiary power was obtained from a small cog wheel operating at the rim of the main water wheel, which presumably drove such small apparatus as bellows, shears, or a grindstone. The supporting corbels for this machinery can be seen inside the walls of the ruin.

Thomas Carfrae's map of 1839 shows the layout of the Fairafar buildings as they originally were. The present square shell, 48 by $43\frac{1}{2}$ feet, inside walls three feet thick, represents the 'west forge' which had two furnaces with chimney stalks and a great tilt hammer. Beside this there stood another building, the 'east forge' under which the lead passed, and from which was removed, on its demolition, the inscribed stone built into the remaining wall, 'B.W.:I.L.:1759'. This forge also housed two furnaces and a hammer. Both buildings are shown quite clearly in an old photograph of the 1920s and behind there are traces of storage for coal and scrap iron sheds built up the slope of the hillside, possibly with first floor loading access by bridge across to the furnace tops. About 50 yards downstream, Mr Alexander Dalrymple recalls there stood a works gatehouse invigilated by the timekeeper. At this point there was clearly a slag tip into the river as accumulations of slag in the river attest. The mill buildings also included a house for the principal forgeman and his family.

Between Fairafar Mill and Cockle Mill there ran, at least as far back as 1839, a tramway or horse railway to facilitate the transport inwards of coal and iron and outwards of the finished iron products. It also served for the transport of stone from the riverside quarries to boats for use in the building of Granton harbour. One of the rails is still to be seen supporting the steps at the waterfall footpath.

The Cockle Mill buildings followed the same general plan as we have seen at Peggie's and Dowie's Mills. Workers' cottages stood against the rising ground. The name of the builder, though wrongly spelt Caddell, is carved into the stonework. Local tradition maintains that the older building adjoining this was erected in the 1740s but a date in the 1760s would seem more acceptable for most of the structures in the area.

On the other side of School Brae the surviving buildings originally included the mill offices, approached by an outside stair. The circular embrasure of the mill clock can still be seen in the wall. Old photographs of about 1900 show this line of buildings as it formerly appeared and the 1860 sale advertisement lists stores, smithies, warehouses and dwellings that stood in this vicinity.

In front of these buildings ran the lead and the railway, the former just visible in one of the photographs. It sprang from the lowest weir, originally 13 feet high, but now half destroyed despite its stone and iron strapping construction, and underpassed the main mill buildings, returning to the river through the culvert in the dock. At the same time the great breast wheel, 18 feet wide, must have spanned the river between the main bank and the constricting weir. The point of entry of its axle may still be seen in the river wall at water level. The mill buildings, apparently already gone by the turn of the century, stood where the car park and green lawn are now laid out. The mill, steam forge, furnaces, stalks, and engine sheds have all disappeared, but the dock survives comparatively intact. Although now silted up, internally it measures 93 feet long, 21 feet wide, and 8 feet deep. This gives some idea of the size of the vessels which it accommodated.

Of the internal arrangements of these mills nothing now remains, and we must rely entirely on verbal descriptions and on contemporary prints of other iron works to give us some idea of the kind of work which went on in this important centre of industry. Of the mill products themselves, we have a few nails and one small iron bar trade-marked with a stag's head, the crest of the Cadell family, and the word 'CRAMOND', rare survivals of a once prolific factory.

NOTES AND REFERENCES

1. Scottish History Society, *Charters of the Abbey of Inchcolm*, ed. Easson and Macdonald, 1938, p. xxi.
2. *Registrum Magni Sigilli*, charters of 1543, 1611, 1620, 1628.
3. Register House, Carron Papers, Cartulary, GD 58 14 1, ff. 1-37.
4. John Kay, *Original Portraits*, vol. 1, p. 225 (Edinburgh 1877).
5. R. H. Campbell, *Carron Company* (Edinburgh 1961), and Henry Hamilton, *Founding of Carron Ironworks* in *Scottish Historical Review* 1908, vol. xxv. It is perhaps worth noting that Hamilton had access to the Carron papers belonging to the Cadell family which Campbell unfortunately did not see.
6. It is possible that John Lee may be referred to in the inscribed date-stone 'B.W.: I.L. 1759', associated with Fairafar Mill.
7. The main source of information for this section is the letterbooks of Carron Company in Register House, GD 58 1 1-11.
8. From this point most information comes from the Cadell family papers and unless otherwise stated quotations are from this source (Acc. 5381 National Library of Scotland).
9. Register House, Cramond Kirk Session Minutes, CH2 246 10.
10. John Philip Wood, *Antient and Modern State of the Parish of Cramond* (Edinburgh 1794).
11. E. T. Svedenstjerna, *Reise duren einen Theil von England und Schottland . . .*, pp. 144-5 (Marburg and Cassel 1811).
12. Henry Hamilton, *The Industrial Revolution in Scotland*, p. 165n. (Oxford 1932).
13. E. T. Svedenstjerna, op. cit.
14. James Mavor, *An Economic History of Russia*, vol. 1, pp. 442, 469 (London and Toronto 1925).
15. Henri Storch, *Tableau Historique et Statistique de L'Empire de Russie à la Fin du dix-huitième Siècle*, vol. 2, pp. 381-401 (Paris 1801).
16. *The Journals, Letters, & Verses of Marjory Fleming*, ed. A. Esdaile, p. 26 (London 1934).
17. I am indebted for this information on Dowie's and Peggie's Mills to Mr W. S. Didcock.
18. Register House, Cramond Heritors' Minutes, HR 713.
19. Census returns for the Parish of Cramond, 1841.
20. Edinburgh Room, Edinburgh Public Libraries, no. 901.

APPENDICES

CRAMOND IN 1782

John Rennie (1761-1821) visited the mills at Cramond in September 1782. Although he was only 21 at the time, Rennie was already a millwright of some distinction. He had been trained under Andrew Meikle, the miller at Saltoun Mill, East Lothian, who was a distinguished mechanical expert in Scotland of his time. He was also studying natural philosophy under Professor Robison at Edinburgh University, earning his fees by doing mill work during the summer holidays. Rennie notices, as Svedenstjerna does later, the amount of iron employed in the actual construction of the mill. This may have been due to the association of Smeaton with Carron Company, as Smeaton is credited with being one of the first millwrights to use metal for pinions. This clearly interested Rennie, and it is worth noting that traditionally it has been customary to think of Rennie's Albion Mills in Southwark as being the first mills to be constructed completely in iron but they were opened four years after this visit. The text comes from a notebook belonging to Rennie which now forms part of the Rennie Papers in the National Library of Scotland (Acc. 5111).

Mills at Cramond.
Rolling Mill

This mill has a water wheel 16f diar & 5f broad the depth of float 11 inches & makes about 16 Revolutions p minute. The whole height of the fall I'm told is 9f of which 6f is stagnate above the apertures of the Sluice. For the other three feet the water descends along a stone lead. The Iron Rollers which are connected with the goudgeon on main axle by means of an hollow Square Iron box they are 18 inches long & 10 diar, thus the rollers makes the same number of revolutions as water wheel.

The frames in which the Rollers moves are cast Iron & are adjusted by means of screws, hence the Rollers are made closser or wider occasionally & consequently the Iron hoop is made thicker or thinner. There is also peices of Iron moveable before the Rollers for guiding the rod & a narrow Spout above with holes in its bottom into which a continued stream of water runs & passes thro' the holes & falls on the Rollers & so keeps them cool.

Forge Mill

The water wheel fall & head is nearly the same as the above. Upon the inner end of the axle is a large Iron collar into which is 6 or 8 square holes for holding wipers to raise the hammer whose weight is 4½ Hd. It makes 120 Strokes p minute, the Stroke being increased by means of a spring beam.

The shaft of the hammer goes into an Iron axle considerably longer on the one side of it than the other; on the long side the frame is moveable & so adjusts the hammer to strike properly on the anvil.

Slit Mill

In this machine there are two water wheels whose dimensions & fall are nearly the same as those already described.

On the axles of each of these wheels is a spur wheel of cast iron acting upon another one of equal size on a lying axle. These water wheels are so placed that the lying axles of the one is directly opposite the principal axle of the other. On the principal axle of the one is a Roller as also on the lying axle of the other & in the same manner a slit roller is on the one axle & lying of the other; by this means there is a pair of Rollers and a Slitting machine drove at once. The Rollers is nearly the same as those formerly described.

The slit wheels is composed of a number of thin plates of steel with pieces of iron between them of such thickness as to make the distance between the steel plates = their thickness or otherwise they are screwed together by means of screwbolts firmly fastened on their goudgeons. Their diar was about 10 inches. These wheels are so placed that the steel plates on the one are opposite the intervals in the other so that the iron after it comes through the rollers is pressed by the slit wheel alternately into each other, so that the size of the iron rod is determined by the thickness of the steel plate.

46

CRAMOND IN 1803

This is a passage from *Resa igenom en del of England och Skottland, åren 1802 och 1803* by Erich Thomas Svedenstjerna who was sent to Britain in 1802 and 1803 by the Swedish Foundry Union to make a study of British methods. This translation is from the German version by Johann Georg Ludolph Blumhof, inspector of factories for the Archduke of Hesse, published as *Reise durch einen Theil von England und Schottland, in den Jahren 1802 und 1803, besonders in berg- und hüttenmännischer, technologischer und mineralogischer Hinsicht,* Marburg and Cassel, 1811, pp. 143-5.

Some miles on another side of Edinburgh is Cramond Iron Works, belonging to Messrs Cadell and Co. It consists of several small works lying on a large stream which is navigable up to the lowest mill but which has several small falls higher up which drive rolling mills, hammers and bellows. No bar iron is made here in the ordinary way. The company simply uses old scrap iron which is worked to order into sheet metal, spades, shovels and the like. This forge work, along with some hundreds of shippounds of steel made in two furnaces from Swedish and Russian iron, seems to be the main production of these works. The works consist of two or three forges, one including a hammer of which the framework wheels and various fittings were constructed in the Swedish manner with this difference that in the six raising levers on the axle of the hammer and in the whole framework of the hammer there was scarcely a piece of wood. Thus the shaft of the hammer was of bar iron in a single piece with the head and had more or less the thickness of a normal shaft. The waterwheels which were undershot, some with upright paddles, some with buckets, were only a few feet high, but were very broad and made of iron and held together with bars of wrought iron. In the same works was a hearth much like our own which was supposed to save a lot of coal, but which also required frequent repairs, even though the cupola was made of very fire resistant stone. This hearth had a pair of large leather bellows driven by water wheels.

A considerable quantity of the scrap iron made into plates here was bought in Holland and consists of old nails, horseshoes, and hundreds of similar things which are collected there partly by the poor in the streets and on the rubbish heaps and partly from old ships and wooden buildings. This old iron along with the trimmings from the sheet metal and the waste from the forges, is laid in so called 'piles' or heaps of 11 or 12 inches each side which are then welded on the bloom furnace or in the previously mentioned hearth before being beaten together under the heavy hammer. The collection of these piles is done by children and old people who are so good at linking the scraps together that the piles can be turned over or roughly handled without losing a single nail. The rolling mill, small and unimportant compared with many others, had a heating furnace and a large set of shears of bar iron with which the iron was cut into plates and spades. At the forge where steel spades and such were drawn the hammer was made in the same way as the other but only weighed 15 or 16 Swedish lispounds and had eight levers. The spade forge which makes an important product operates something like this. After the sheet metal destined for spades had been cut into suitable lengths and breadths they were drawn under the small hammer to 7″ by 4″ by ⅛″ thick. They were then taken to the small forge where they were laid together two by two linked by a piece of scrap steel at the blade end. Sand or earth was sprinkled over the other end so as to prevent welding of the spot where the handle was to be joined to the blade. They were then brought back to the hammer where they were drawn to 13″ by 7″ by scarcely 1/12″. After this operation they were taken for a second time to the small forge where they were finally cut, rough filed, hammered cold, and provided with hardwood handles. A dozen of them were sold on the spot for £2. These spades which can be got all over England and Scotland are about the size of our sand shovels but not quite as long and somewhat smaller towards the blade which is quite straight. I have no doubt that these spades could be better and cheaper made at home if there were a market for them.

APPENDIX 3

CRAMOND IN 1855

This description of the mills in January 1855 is really no more than a memorandum by Henry Cadell to his copartners giving them an idea of the improved output to be expected from the introduction of a new steam engine, an event which had taken place the year before. It gives incidentally a lot of information about the amount of iron produced in the early 1850s and about the performance of a steam engine in the production of iron goods. In the event the memorandum was excessively optimistic.

Remarks upon the State of the Rolling Mill
& Forge at Cramond & the produce of Iron hitherto
manufactured & estimated capability, by Henry
Cadell Jany 1855.

The Works previous to the erection of the Steam Engine (last year) are at the two lowest falls upon the river Almond. At the lowest, the Cockle Mill, there was a Breast Water Wheel of 18 feet in breadth & 14 feet diameter taking in the whole river in its ordinary state & estimated at 35 horses power which drove:—

 1 train 14 inch rolls at 90 & 70 rev p m.
 1 train 9 inch grinders.
 1 patent shingler of (?) 6 f dia.
 1 shears for 14 in train, 1 shears for grinder.
 To these we appended
 2 heating furnaces.
 2 puddling furnaces.

The Puddle bar and finishing rolls were both in one train, and the water wheel could drive only one train of rolls at one time, being generally wrought one shift upon Puddle bar & Faggoting, the other upon finishing.

At the Forge (Fairafar) there are
1 Water Wheel undershot driving a helve hammer for shingling and heavy forgings.
1 Water Wheel undershot driving a hammer for light forgings.
1 Small Wheel overshot driving a shears and grindstone.

The first has two heating furnaces attached & is used generally one shift in forging blooms from scraps (in the 2 furnaces), & the other shift on forgings with a single furnace, the other to heat light forgings has 2 Chafferies, one of which is wrought at a time.

49

The Water Wheels have, especially of late years, been subject to frequent interruptions from Spets in the Winter season and from want of water in the Summer, besides which the Cockle (or Rolling) Mill wheel being placed about 9 feet under high water of spring tides was subject to an interruption every 12 hours of from 3 to 5 hours.

The quantity of finished Iron and forgings made in the last nine years as taken from the Ledger in which is included a small quantity bought in, has been:—

	tons	cw	q	lb
Year ending 30 June 1846	1164	7	1	5
1847	1000	13	–	19
1848	1022	3	1	5
1849	827	15	2	14
1850	867	7	3	17
1851	912	4	3	4
1852	1023	16	2	2
1853	1155	9	3	4
1854	1151	5	1	
in all	9125	3	2	14.

being on an average 84½ tons p month.

The bar iron & forgings being both together in the account, in order to find the proportion due to each, I have taken the year ending 30 June 1854 in which the disposal of Bar Iron was 719 14 2 17
of forgings 399 12 2 4
in all 1119 7 21
Being on an average Bar Iron 60 tons p month
Forgings 33
93

The erection of an engine to drive the machinery at the Cockle Mill has superseded the Water Wheel which besides being such a bad power for Working Iron was completely done, & broke down completely in July last 2 months before the steam engine could be started. This Engine is 50 horses power, being a high pressure engine, cylr 26 inch with 4 feet stroke, & when well kept in steam goes easily driving all the machinery. At present there are three boilers 6 feet diameter & 15 feet over the hemispherical ends, wrought from the waste heat of 2 heating & 1 Puddling Furnace. When going upon large sizes of iron these are nearly sufficient to keep the engine going, but when working upon small sizes in which a great deal of motion is required without much firing in the furnaces they are far deficient in the supply of steam, and another boiler has been ordered to be wrought from the waste heat of the two remaining Puddling Furnaces, which it is fully expected will keep the Engine amply supplied with steam.

In order to work advantageously, and that the least possible waste of fewel & material should take place both the Finishing Mill and Puddling should be carried on regularly on both shifts, and with this trim the addition of a set of rough rolls & a shears will be necessary to render the arrangement complete.

The produce of iron should then be of Rough Iron by Puddle bar & blooms at Mill 3 Puddling Furnaces, 2 shifts   6 tons

               1 Ball   Furnace 1   3

           Forge 2 Ball furnaces   1   7

in all per day   16

being p week (5 da) 80 tons, or p An 4000 tons.

          Finished Iron.

at Mill   14 inch mill   1 shift 7 tons

           9" Grinder   1   4

   Forge Forgings $3\frac{1}{2}$

in all per day $14\frac{1}{2}$

being $72\frac{1}{2}$ tons p week (5 da) or 3625 tons p An.

With the small produce of iron hitherto made, from the rent of the Mill & permanent charges being heavy compared with the output, the cost of production is high. I will place in contrast the cost of producing with an output of $84\frac{1}{2}$ tons p month what it has been for the last nine years, and with the quantity calculated viz. 312 tons p month which I am satisfied may quite easily be done if the work is at all managed, and it may here be noticed that the difficulty hitherto has not been in getting orders but in the executing of them.

The cost of producing hitherto may be stated thus taking the present price of scraps & coals viz.

1st Process Blooms or Scrap rough bars:

22 cwts scraps	@ 5/	£5:10	
Coals for heatg—15 cwt 9/ 2/ [?transport]	11/	£-: 8:3	
Wages, Heating, Shingling		£-:10:-	
Rent & Charges		£-:10:-	
Cost of Blooms &c p ton		£6:18:3.	

2 Process finishing scrap Bars:

22 cwt blooms or rough bar	@ 138/	£7:11:9
Coals 13½ cwt	@ 11/	7:4
Wages, Rollers 4/2, Heater 2/2, Shearg 1/8		8
Rent & Charges		10
Cost of Scrap Bars pr ton		£8:17:1.

————Common Iron————

1st Process, making puddle bars:

22½ cwt Pig or cast scraps	@ 3/6	£3:18:9.
Coals 1 ton		11
Wages Puddler 10/ 5/6 2/		17:6
Rent & Charges		10
Cost of Puddle bar per ton		£5:17:3.

2 Process, Finishing Common Iron——

22 cwt Puddle bar	@ 117/3	£6:9
Coals, heating 13½ cwt	@ 11/	7:4
Wages of Roller &c		8
Rent & Charges		10
Cost of Common Iron p ton		£7:14:4.

——Forgings——

24 cwt Blooms or rough &c bars:

as before	@ 138/3	£8:5:11
Coals 15 cwt	11/	8:3
Wages, Forgemen		15:10
Rent & Charges		10
		£10:

These rates are taken at the present prices and of course when the price of material & wages is low there will be a proportionate difference. As however the price of scraps, coals, and wages generally fall along with the price of iron, there should be a proportionate margin over when the price is low. The price as above for producing scrap bars is   £8:17:1

to which add carriage to Edr	4:11
	9: 2
Selling price £11:10 to £12:10 say	12
Profit on scrap bars	2:18

Common Iron £7:14:4, carriage 4/8	£7:19
Selling price £10 to £11:10 say	10:10
Profit on Comn Iron	2:11

Forgings, axles, plough beams, socks	£10
Selling Price	13:10
Profit on forgings	3:10

It may now be remarked that that with a small output the rent & permanent charges in the Works fall very heavy as a charge in the tons of iron produced.

The rent rated on the mill p an is	£420
on the forge	100
Charges for Yr endg 30 June 1854	699:4
Interest on borrowed money	259:16
Total independent of D's debts (£150)	1479

This rated upon the limited output hitherto, say last year 1119 tons, came to £1:6:6 per ton whereas were the produce brought up to what it should now be 3625 tons p an it would only be 8/2 per ton, besides which under the present, or late, system the Furnaces have to be firing in for 12 hours of the 24 thereby occasioning a great unnecessary waste of fewel which cannot be taken at less than 5/ per ton of iron produced.

In order to render the improvement effected by the erection of the Steam Engine complete, & that the work may be carried on to the best advantage some additions will yet be requisite viz: at the Mill—one set Puddlers rolls and one pair shears—these can now readily be put up, and their expense would be repaid in six months. At the Forge as the helve hammer is ill adapted to heavy forgings but answers well for shingling scraps, I would recommend that it should be kept regularly in at shingling & which being done regularly in place of any alternate shift will effect a considerable saving in fuel—and would erect a steam hammer for the forging of heavy work, which besides making a better job of the forgings would get through treble the work at a far less cost per ton.

Dalkeith.

Jany 1855.   Henry Cadell.

There then follows another shorter note regarding the saving to be made, as follows:

From the foregoing calculations of prices it will be seen that there should have been a considerable profit upon last years transactions (from 1 July 1853 to 30 June 1854) trade having been very good all the time and no interruptions of any consequence having taken place during the year. The disposal of Bar Iron during the year was as before mentioned 719 tons; of this there might be

			cost
Scrap Iron	369 making p ton £8:17:6	£3274:17:6
Common	350	7:15:0	2712:10
& Forgings	399	10	3990
			£9977:7:6.

(In Ledger in Dt side of bar iron a/c as made is £12765:1:1)

The selling price of these after making allowance for discounts &c:

Scrap Iron	369 tons @ £12		£4428
Common	350	10:10	3675
Forgings	399	13:10	5368:10
	1118		13471:10
From which deduct makg cost			9977:7:6
which leaves as profit			3493:2:6

(In L at Cr side of bar iron a/c as disposed of is 1153 tons: £14410:11:4.)

The profits actually realised as shown by the balance sheet were in all £932:6:11, of this there were upon paper:

Making	£203:5:11	
Store	266:6:6	
Balance of profit of last year	150	
Spades & Shovels, Nails &c	147:13:5	767:5:10
which fall to be deducted from the gross profit	£165:1:1.

Leaves as the profit upon the Iron Making department of the works: £165: 1:1—How this state of matters has arisen, has not yet been accounted for but surely it is high time that something was done to remedy such an abuse.

WORKMEN EMPLOYED AT CRAMOND IRON WORKS 1767

This is a list, in Edington's hand, of the workmen employed at the Cramond Iron Works in November 1767. It also includes details of pay, and some indication of the work done.

List of Workmen at Slittmill 12 Novr 1767.

Joshua Padmore Slitter	17/	a week.
James Cruickshanks Apprentice	5/	do.
Hugh Kennedy Furnaceman	9/	do.
John McCurrie Midleman	6/	do.
Jas. Martin Carpenter & Cutterman	8/	do.

These we employ constantly.

Wm. McCurrie Furnaceman	6/	a week.
James Lowney Midleman	6/	do.
D. Stephenson Cutterman	6/	do.

These three are only employed during the Winter Season when we are plenty of Water.

James Bleckie Hoop Bundler; when he is not employed at that he makes Sadd Iron Handles. For the Hoops he get ½d pr Bundle & 4½d pr lib for the Handles.

We also employ boys to Streight Hoops at 1d pr Bundle.

Rob. Symons	6/	a week.
John Grindlay	6/	do.

These two I employed to quarry stones for Damhead, but for some days I have made them Bundle Iron in the day, & so wrought both furnaces in the Day & one furnace in the night.

Padmore is now to have 2/ a week for Teaching the apprentice.

Wm McCurrie is to get 1/ a week more should he work the Furnaces to my satisfaction.

James McCurrie goes with the letters three times a week to Edinr & any other errands he has 2/6 a week.

WORKMEN AT CRAMOND 1792, 1841, 1851, 1861

The list of 1792 is that supplied by Dr Robert Spotswood for J. P. Wood, who was then in the process of compiling his history of the parish of Cramond.

Millmen:
Donald Corbet
Alexander Gunn
William Henderson
Andrew Hill
John Hutton
James Lowney sen.
James Lowney jun.
Kenneth MacKenzie
William MacKenzie
Alexander Simons
John Stuart
John Walker

Slitters:
John MacAra
James Cruickshanks (assistant)

Carters:
William Ritchie sen.
William Ritchie jun.

Carpenter:
John Stuart

Foregemen:
James McAra
Thomas McAra
William Probert sen.
William Probert jun.
J. Henderson (assistant)
C. Probert (assistant)

Nailers:
C. Burkley

Nailers (cont.):
J. Gould
J. Jackson
M. Jackson
J. Jamieson
Alexander Jenkins
William Kilgour
J. Marshall
William Marshall
R. Russin
C. Willis

Labourers:
James Cameron sen.
James Cameron jun.
James Gibson
James Hutton
D. McIntosh
R. Monro
Thomas Myles
James Whyte

Spademakers:
Richard Squires (foreman)
H. Black
James Black
G. Cleland
J. Henderson
R. Hill
John Mawers
Alexander White

Masons:
James Crawford
R. Moubray
James West

Boys:
   12 working at nails
   7 drawing and straighting hoops
   2 with the forgemen
   1 apprentice to the slitter

Spadeshaftmakers:
   William Plain and three others.

This gives a total workforce of 78 men and boys, though John Stuart the carpenter may also be John Stuart the millman. Richard Squires is more usually known as Richard Squair. The forgeman James McAra was transported in 1811 for the murder of his brother Alexander with a pair of furnace tongs at the slit mill. Marjory Fleming notes the event in her diary, and it is largely written up in the *Scots Magazine* for that year.

From 1841 the census returns have survived and it is possible to gain a more complete picture of the men who were employed at Cramond. The census was taken at people's homes, and the arrangement therefore is according to place of dwelling rather than according to their work. Many of the functions, such as 'roller' or 'furnaceman', clearly indicate a person employed at the iron works. The terms 'wright' or 'blacksmith' are much less precise. On the whole wrights, blacksmiths and masons have been left out unless there is some obvious reason for supposing them to have been employed at the mills. They have been included, for example, if they lived actually at the mill or if they were born in England which usually indicates that they were recruited for the mill. Partners and managers are also omitted as they were not included by either Edington or Spotswood.

Arrangement is by domicile and then by alphabetical order. The name comes first followed by age, function and place of birth in that order. If there is no entry under place of birth, the person in question was born in the parish of Cramond.

1841.

Three names marked with an asterisk were also employed in 1792.

Cramond Village:

Robert Atkinson	40 papermaker	England
William Baillie	40 nailer	
Robert Buchan	40 millwright	Scotland
James Conway	37 ironparer	England
Alexander Dalrymple	35 blacksmith	
James Dalrymple	19 puddler	
Anthony Douglas	15 apprentice millwright	
John Douglas	56 millwright	
Robert Douglas	26 forgeman	
Alexander Goodlet	56 millwright	
William Gray	25 labourer (papermill)	

John Henderson	25 journeyman spademaker	
Philip Lumley	33 turner England	
Margaret McDonald	30 papermaker	
Angus McKinnon	35 labourer Scotland	
James McUrich	18 forgeman	
John Marr	69 spademaker	
William Orr	37 labourer	
George White	17 labourer	Total: 19 (1 woman)

Cockle Mill:

William Addison	24 roller England	
Adam Allan	29 hammerman Scotland	
James Arthur	40 stocktaker Scotland	
Charles Barklay	55 furnaceman	
Peter Bisset	20 furnaceman	
James Bowater	35 mill foreman England	
John Bowater	25 roller England	
Alexander Brown	15 puddler	
Charles Brown	23 blacksmith	
David Brown	25 puddler	
Gideon Brown	75 labourer	
John Brown	25 spademaker	
William Brown	20 millwright	
Samuel Conway	64 roller England	
John Glennie	20 smith	
George Herdman	18 apprentice blacksmith	
William Herdman	55 blacksmith Scotland	
James Hutton	14 forgeboy	
Richard Hutton	54 forgeman Scotland	
Agnes Kerr	20 labourer Scotland	
Ann Kerr	15 labourer	
Mary Kerr	25 labourer Scotland	
*Thomas McAra	70 hammerman	
William McAra	30 hammerman	
Robert Marr	35 labourer	
*Charles Probert	63 steelmaker Scotland	
Joseph Rabone	25 puddler England	
Francis Smith	72 blacksmith England	
John Smith	40 blacksmith England	
Bill Walker	17 spademaker England	
Nicolas Walker	14 apprentice roller England	
Adam White	30 forgeman	
William White	25 forgeman	Total: 33 (3 women)

Fairafar Forge:

Thomas Dods	29 furnaceman	
Alexander White	60 furnaceman	Total: 2

57

Peggie's Mill:
Alexander Hill	60	papermaker	
George Hill	20	journeyman papermaker	
James Hill	15	stationer	Total: 3

Dowie's Mill:
Andrew Aird	23	spadehandlemaker	Scotland
Thomas Aird sen.	44	spadehandlemaker	Scotland
Thomas Aird jun.	14	spadehandlemaker	Scotland
Charles Aitchison sen.	50	papermaker	
Charles Aitchison jun.	14	apprentice spademaker	
James Aitchison	11	papermaker	
Alexander Aitken	28	papermaker	
Thomas Aitken	25	papermaker	
John Gothard	23	spademaker	England
Thomas Gothard	43	spademaker	England
Robert Henderson	60	spademaker	Scotland
George Hunter sen.	49	chainmaker	England
George Hunter jun.	14	apprentice chainmaker	
William Hunter	16	apprentice chainmaker	England
Robert Lumley	49	spademaker	England
Alexander Mathewson	30	papermaker	
John Saunderson	33	spademaker	
James Scully	18	papermaker	Ireland
George Stobbart	40	forgeman	England
Henry Stobbart	19	spademaker	England
James Wauch	12	apprentice papermaker	
John Wauch	20	papermaker	
Robert Wauch	14	apprentice papermaker	
William Wauch	45	papermaker	
*Charles Willis	70	nailer	
Charles Willis jun.	35	nailer	
George Willis	30	nailer	
Thomas Willis	25	nailer	Total: 28

Elsewhere:
William Farquar	45	labourer	
James Hamilton	24	labourer	Total: 7
John Henderson	46	labourer	These appear to have
William Henderson	26	labourer	been mostly single men
John Hervey	13	labourer	living in lodgings, the
Thomas Hill	40	nailer	majority of them in
Alexander Mitchell	18	labourer	Davidson's Mains.

The total labour force in 1841 seems to have been 94 with an average age of 32 of whom four were women, and 13 were under 16 years of age. It is possible that some workers lived outside the parish, and it is also possible that the Aird family who ran the saw mill at Dowie's Mill should not be counted with the employees of the works as they did work for outsiders and were themselves employers of labour.

1851.

One person, Charles Willis, marked with a dagger, was employed in 1792.

Twenty-seven people marked with an asterisk were also employed in 1841.

Cramond Village:

*Robert Atkinson	50 papermaker	England
John Baillie	26 furnaceman	
*Charles Barclay	65 nailer	
James Bisset	34 furnaceman	
George Borthwick	29 labourer	Dalmeny
Lawrence Dow	37 traveller	North Leith
James Goodlet	31 engineer	
*William Gray	40 labourer (papermaker)	Edinburgh
William McUrich	17 labourer	
Catherine Morrison	18 ragcutter	
Charles Morrison	21 roller	
Margaret Morrison	16 scrap picker	
George Sanderson	17 malleable iron maker	
*John Sanderson sen.	42 nailer	
John Sanderson jun.	22 malleable iron maker	
†Charles Willis	80 labourer	
*Thomas Willis	37 labourer	Total: 17 (2 women)

Cockle Mill:

*William Addison	33 roller	England
*Peter Bisset	31 furnaceman	
*David Brown	34 malleable iron worker	
William Brown	16 labourer	
Isabella Conway	16 scrap picker	
*James Conway	47 shearer	
William Conway	18 labourer	
*Alexander Dalrymple	44 blacksmith	
Thomas Dalrymple	15 engine keeper	
Jane Glenny	45 paperpicker	
Margaret Glenny	25 paperpicker	
James Henderson	56 labourer	
Walter Herdman	23 blacksmith	
*William Herdman	67 blacksmith	
*Richard Hutton	64 forgeman	Kilsyth
Richard Hutton jun.	21 forgeman	
William Lindsay	29 provision storekeeper	Glasgow

*William McAra sen. 40 hammerman
William McAra jun. 16 hammerman
*Robert Marr 46 shearer
Robert Mitchell 36 engineer Aberdeen
*William Orr 47 labourer (coalheaver) Ratho
William Probert 14 forgeman's assistant
*Joseph Rabone 37 malleable iron maker England
Henry Ranstead 20 forgeman
John Ranstead 18 spademaker
George Turner 34 roller England
Joseph Walker 22 labourer
*Adam White 42 blacksmith
*William White 31 forgeman
James Whiteford 24 malleable iron worker Kirkliston
William Whiteford 22 roller Total: 32 (3 women)

Fairafar:
John Eadon 42 steel filer England Total: 1

Peggie's Mill:
John Fulton 17 apprentice papermaker
Jane Johnston 26 rag cutter
Janet Waugh 32 rag cutter Currie
*William Waugh 57 papermaker Pennycuik Total: 4 (2 women)

Dowie's Mill:
*Thomas Aird sen. 54 spadehandlemaker and woodmerchant Ayton
*Thomas Aird jun. 23 spadehandlemaker Livingstone
*Charles Aitchison 63 papermaker Pennycuik
*Alexander Aitken 38 papermaker Colinton
Peter Creamer 33 labourer Ireland
John Gothard 32 spademaker England
Thomas Gothard 54 spademaker England
*Robert Henderson 73 spademaker Inverkeithing
Archibald Hunter 17 chainmaker
*George Hunter 59 chainmaker England
John Lumley 12 papermaker
*Robert Lumley 59 spademaker England
John McAuring 12 labourer Ireland
Michael McAuring 15 paper sorter Ireland
Owen McAuring 31 labourer Ireland
Francis McGovern 15 paper sorter Ireland
Thomas McGovern 46 labourer Ireland
Thomas Thomson 26 spadehandlemaker Leith
Thomas Ward 35 spademaker England Total: 19

Elsewhere:
*Thomas Hill   50 nailer
William Semple   42 labourer   Total: 2

This gives a total labour force of 75, with an average age of just over 34, of whom 7 were women and 6 under 16. There are more women than in 1841, but fewer boys, and the labour force, perhaps with the refounding of the company has been considerably reduced.

1861.

Three people marked with a dagger were also employed in 1841 but not in 1851.

Ten people marked with a double asterisk were also employed in 1841 and 1851.

Nine people marked with a single asterisk were also employed in 1851.

Cramond Village:
Charles Baillie   31 labourer
William Baillie   62 hammerman Annan
Agnes Barclay   17 ragpicker Old Monkland
**Charles Barclay   75 nailer (pauper)
Charles Barclay   16 papermaker
David Barclay   49 roller
James Barclay   14 papermaker
Christina Brown   40 ragpicker
†John Brown   45 spademaker St Cuthberts
Primrose Haig   19 papermaker (this was a man)
†Philip Lumley   53 blacksmith England
*Robert Lumley   24 roller England
Alexander McGowan 58 traveller Bannockburn
William McGowan   19 clerk Stirling
James Marshall   48 fireman Abernethy
James Roberts   29 steam hammer driver Haddington
David Willis   18 ironmoulder Greenock Total: 17 (2 women)

Cockle Mill:
Thomas Addison   14 labourer
**William Addison   42 roller England
Adam Allan   45 ball furnaceman Duns
William Allan   17 labourer Duns
William Barclay   27 storekeeper Johnston
**David Brown   42 puddler Lasswade
*James Conway   57 shearer Wales
Peter Coutts   38 machine fitter St Andrews
†James Dalrymple   38 puddler
George Eadon   20 roller England
*James Goodlet   42 engineer
**Richard Hutton   74 forgeman Kilsyth

Robert Johnston	23	machine fitter Longside (Aberdeenshire)
James Lindsay	35	millwright Uddingston
Elizabeth Lothian	43	scrappicker
John McKenzie	48	labourer Crathie
Lewis McKenzie	42	clerk Crathie
David Maxwell	39	machine fitters' labourer
*Charles Morrison	31	roller
Alexander Noble	25	machine fitter Gujerat
**William Orr	57	weigher Ratho
William Whyte	27	machine fitter Cupar Total 22: (1 woman)

Fairafar:

William McUrich	22	hammerman
*William Semple	52	weigher Total: 2

Peggie's Mill:

**Robert Atkinson	60	papermaker England Total: 1

Dowie's Mill:

**Thomas Aird	64	woodmerchant (employing 6 men and 2 boys) Berwick on Tweed
**Alexander Aitken	50	papermaker Colinton
Ann Aitken	14	paperpicker Ireland
Helen Aitken	21	paperpicker Ireland
Mary Aitken	19	paperpicker Ireland
Michael Aitken	55	papermaker Edinburgh
Thomas Aitken	18	papermaker
*John Gothard	43	spademaker
*Thomas Gothard	63	spademaker England
Thomas Gothard	20	spadeshaftmaker
Henry Grant	27	labourer Bathgate
Isabella Grant	54	labourer Falkirk
William Grant	51	labourer Kirkliston
James Gray	18	papermaker
George Haig	23	papermaker
Jane Haig	23	papermaker
James Henderson	27	spademaker
James Hill	60	papermaker Durham
John Kerr	26	spadeplater Bothwell
*John Lumley	22	spademaker England
**Robert Lumley	69	spademaker England
William McArthur	17	spademaker
*Francis McGovern	26	papermaker Ireland
Brian McQueen	38	labourer Ireland
John McQueen	13	labourer Ireland
Henry Stobart	16	turner Edinburgh
William Thomson	29	turner Crail

Alison Will	42	paperpicker	Pennycuik	
John Will	67	papermaker	Lasswade	
**Thomas Willis	47	labourer		Total: 30 (6 women)

Elsewhere:

Peter Rodger	44	carter	Gladsmuir	
George James Wilson	21	iron manufacturer	Glasgow	Total: 2

This gives a total work force of 74 with an average age of nearly 37, of whom 9 were women and 4 under the age of 16. It should perhaps be noted that the four machine fitters (Coutts, Johnston, Noble and Whyte) who were living at Cockle Mill are described as lodgers.

DETAILS OF POPULATION OF CRAMOND IN 1792

	Population	Families	Farmers	Weavers	Smiths	Wrights	Coopers	Gardeners	Shoemakers	Masons	Seamen	Brewers	Bakers	Tailors	Butchers	Turners	Tanners	Episcopalians	Anabaptists	Seceders	Glassies	French Calvinists	Horses	Cattle	Sheep
Barony of Leny	126	30	6	6		2	2																38	44	100
New Saughton	55	6							3														14	8	90
Braehead	50	13		2		2			3														14	13	
Barnton Nook	6	1						1																	
North Clermiston	9	2							1														6	3	
Cadell and Edington	39	9																							
Robt. Spotswood, Bayn White	25	6	1																				6	7	
Southfield and Fairafar	49	7		2																			25	14	
Craigcrook	54	14					1			2													18	16	
Nether Cramond	343	87	1			14		2	2	7	18	1	1	6			2	5					15	25	50
Barony of Cramond	108	31	3	3		3		2							2	1							31	25	10
Barnton	146	28	2	4				7												4			39	27	100
Lauriston	99	24	1	4				1							1		1						20	10	
Muirhouse	78	14	3	3				1							1					3			37	22	
Pilton	62	10	3																1				21	7	
Drylaw	154	31	3	3	1	2			1														38	19	
Royston and Granton	88	?16	1	1					1					1				6		6		1	27	14	40
Totals	1491	339	26	10	13	27	1	16	6	16	18	11	1	9	1	1	9	9	9	9	1	1	350	238	380

REMARKS ON EXPENSES OF CRAMOND 1765-6

There is a draft memorandum in the hand of William Cadell on expenses at Cramond and on what should be done to keep them down. It gives an interesting picture of the difficulties encountered at Cramond and should be compared with Appendix 8 which gives the expenses at Cramond for the calendar year 1766. The dots in the text were put in by Cadell himself, who regularly used dots in that way instead of more normal punctuation.

Remarks on the Expence . . . & Work done at Crammond
fro March 1st 1765 to March 1st 1766.

The advance at Crammond has unexpectedly increased during the last Year from £2459:12/7 to £2776:15/10 . . . the following are what at present occurr to us as part, if not the whole of the causes of this disagreeable advance.

·In April a scarcity of Russian Iron made us attempt to roll Plate Iron from 4 to 12 inches broad for the London Sale. The shortness of the Rollers . . . & weakness of every part of the Machinery, after repeated Trials for 3 or 4 Weeks made us give up the attempt . . . after hurting the Machinery very much & losing 30 or £40 to the mill.

The Mill was this year loaded with 3 years' Feuduty (extra) owing Sir John Inglis preceding 1764. £64 which with about £40 of other old accos made an extra addition of £100 on this years Transactns.

Repairing the Damhead . . . converting the Blade Mill into a mill for turning the Rollers . . . and building a new shop has been an additionall expence of £60 to £80.

The Expence . . . & Loss by Turning . . . & breaking of bad Rollers, has been an additl Expce & Waste of time, equal to £40 or £50. This it is probable (from what we now see) will be effectually prevented in time to come by casting them in Loam with large heads to make them solid.

The great want of Water by the uncommon drought in Summer & Frost in Winter almost put an intire stop to the business at Crammond for 3 or 4 Months . . . wch together with the loss by the Weakness and Failure of the Machinery caused a very great Loss to the Mill.

The expence of Labour at Crammond owing to the great Number of hands imployed wch is partly occasioned by the scarcity of the Water & frequent interruptions by Land Floods . . . and Tides . . . wch makes it necessary to imploy a Double Sett of hands, when otherways a single Sett would be sufficient for our Quantity of Work yearly, being about

400 tons of Rod Iron & 100 Tons of Hoops . . . & partly by the want of Skill & exertion of our Mill Men . . . who take five men for a Sett in place of Three as in Staffordshire.

It is determined to put in Two able Wheells this Summer wch will give the Mill a much greater power than formerly . . . when that is done with the assistance of an able Mill Man from Staffordshire . . . & good assistants, that notwithstanding the many Natural disadvantages at Crammond it will be found practicable . . . with a double Sett consisting of 8 hands to Slitt & role 600 Ton of Rods . . . & 200 Tons of Hoops a year . . . or with a single Sett of 4 & the assistance of 4 additionall 3 Months in winter . . . 400 Tons of Rods & 100 Ton of Hoops . . . at following Expence. . . .

Clerk	£35.
Slitter & Apprentice. 21/	52:10
Principall Millman. 12/	30
3 Assistts . . . 12 Mos at £20	60
4 additiol . . . 4 Mos	20
1 Labourer for Iron & Coals	13
1 Boy for errands &c	6
Carpenter	20
for 400 rods . . . 100 hps	£236:10
Coal for Mill Houses & Shops	100
Feuduty	21:1
Timber . . . Iron . . . Grease . . . Soap . . .	
Candles . . . Rollers . . . Repairs . . .	
Utensils . . . & petty Expces . . . I	
fear will not be brot under	200
Bundelg & straightg Hoops	25
	£582:11
Additional if 600 Rds & 200 Hps . . .	
Labour	£60
Coal	60
Reprs & Petty Expces	80
	£782:11.

If it is not convenient for Mr Garbett to part with the Mill Man now at Crammond . . . we should lose no time in seeing for a very able Mill Man from Staffordshire, who should be strictly bound not to work for any other Slitt Mill in Scotland.

In the South end of the Ware at Crammond . . . by the Sluices . . . Foundations and ends of the Mills a large quantity of Water is lost in

Dry weather. T.E. is desired to consult a person of Skill about the most frugall . . . & effectual means of stopping the water . . . and to send us an estimate of the expence . . . if it comes within any moderate compass it should certainly be done. T.E. is also desired to keep his accot of Cash paid out so as we may at the end of every year see at one view the amount of every separate Expce Accot . . . Slitter's Wages . . . Mill Men . . . Labourers . . . Coals . . . Timber . . . Iron . . . Candles, . . . Greese . . . Soap . . . Rollers . . . Repairs . . . Utensils & Incidental Expences . . . by which we may the more readily judge what articles can & what cannot admitt of reduction.

APPENDIX 8

EXPENSES OF CRAMOND 1766

A note of expenses at Cramond for the year 1766 is in the hand of William Cadell. The figures of wages for the workmen are of course weekly wages, and the final total of £565:7s represents the total expenditure in that year not including the actual iron used. It looks as though Cadell has included twice the sum of £120 for incidental expenses. It should be noticed that the amount of work done in this year, 300 tons of rod iron and 100 tons of hoops, is less than that projected the previous March and the actual expense of doing it is only about £17 less.

	Computatn. Expence at Cramnd.	
1 Fireman	9/	
1 Midlemn	7/	
3 assists & bundlers	18/	
allowces	6/	
	40/	£104.
Slittrs Appce		60
Coals . . . 250 Tns . . . @ 8/		100
Labourers . . . 2 @ jobs weighg & deliverg Goods		30
Clerk		30
Streighg & bundg hoops		30
Carpentr		20
Rent or Feuduty		21:7
Soap Candles & Greese		50
Cast Iron . . . Steell . . . Iron Cuttrs . . . Plates . . . Utensils & Repairs		120
		£565:7.

Slitt Mills at Crammond   Decr 1766.

420 Tons Russian & other Iron at			Sale. . . .	
£14:15. . . .		£6195.		
Slitting 300 Tons Rod Iron at 21/ £315			300 Tons Rod Iron at 19/	
100 Hoops 50/ 250	565			£5700
Proportion of Generl Expences	120		100 Hoops 21/	2100
	£7800			£7800.

Ballance £920.

SUPPLY OF IRON 1778

William Cadell has left a record of the iron it had been agreed to buy for the year 1778. It gives a good idea of the way in which Cramond spread its purchases in Britain and in Russia. In fact there are only six Russian mines mentioned in this list, though at various times Cramond had iron from many more.

Import . . . from Atkins & Co . . . 60 Tons Gurieffs
                                     140   other sorts . . . viz.
                                              Govermt. $2\frac{1}{4}$ by $\frac{5}{8}$ in.
                                                do.   common Sizes.
                                              Brinsky, Gleboffs or
                                              Twerdisheffs.

N.B. is Government common Bars   Scrap Iron
as Tough for Hoops & Bolts.   Squares if at under £12:10
                                              at Petersburg.

Sutherland & Co. . . .   30 to 40 Tons Ivan Demidoffs if at or
                                              under 72 Cos.
                                              for Rolling, Rod Iron or
                                              Squaring.

London . . . in return for steel & other Goods   100 Tons for Hoops
                                              Rods & Rolling.

Leith. . . . Mr Jameson 70 ⎫ 140 Tons Government or Gurieffs
          Mr Pillans   35 ⎬   answer for Steel Hoops or
          Mr Sibbald   35 ⎭   Rods.
Carron
& accidental purchases on easy terms 120

                                              Tns
                                            300 Rods
                                            200 Hoops
                                            100 Steel &c
                                            ———
                                            600.

Ord. Iron from Meml [Memel] &c   50
Iron from Gottg [Gothenburg]   30
Scrap Iron   30
                                            ———
                                         710 Tons.

It would be agreeable to have the Iron delivered at times suitable for the works.

TECHNICAL TERMS USED BY THE COMPANY 1778

This list comes from a copy of a letter of Thomas Edington to William Hood the Cramond Company's London agent who had been very much mystified by the technical terms used by the company especially with regard to hoops and rod iron. The letter is dated 10 May 1778.

NAMES & DIMENSIONS OF HOOPS 1778

Spanish or plate hoops:	1 inch broad & very thinn Rolled—when an order is received for Hoops to be sent to Spain Portugall or Madeira it should be execute of the following lengths viz—
SPAIN & PORTUGALL	$\frac{1}{2}$ the quantity to be 7 feet 11 inches
	$\frac{1}{4}$ 8 feet 4 In
	$\frac{1}{4}$ 9 feet 1 In

about 56 Bund. of these makes a Ton in Manufacturing Plate. Hoops we cannot avoid making a great many shorter or longer then these lengths, which we get free of by sending them to Country & other Dealers who do not limit us to lengths—Note that in executing an order for Spain or Portugall Hoops 6 or 8 inches longer than the above may be sent but none shorter.

MADEIRA HOOPS	1 inch broad same as the plate Hoops
	$\frac{1}{2}$ the quantity 6$\frac{1}{2}$ feet long.
	$\frac{1}{4}$ 7$\frac{1}{2}$ feet do.
	$\frac{1}{4}$ 8 feet do.

about 60 Bundles or 1200 pieces of these Hoops makes a Ton; when Rivetts are ordered send the same number as there is pieces of Hoops & Charge 5d pr lb.

COOPERS OR RUMPUNCHEON HOOPS 1$\frac{1}{4}$ Inch broad are used in large quantitys by the Coopers in London & by Country dealers & are made in lengths from 6 to 10 feet. They are also exported to the West Indies & called Rumpuncheon at the following lengths—

Head Hoops	8 feet	
Quarter do.	8$\frac{1}{2}$	3 bundles of 8 feet to be sent to 2 of any other size
Bulge	9	
Some few	9$\frac{1}{2}$	

about 40 bundles of these lengths make a Ton—Coopers Hoops are also used for Hhds [hogsheads] in the following lengths

Head Hoop	6 feet 5 inches	In executing Country orders where the lengths are not fixed send such as will not do for Puncheon or Hhds; lengths which are always limited not to be shorter.
Quarter do.	6 feet 9 in	
Bulge do.	7 feet 3 in.	
some few about 6 feet, 5 feet 8 ins, & 5 feet		

COOPERS PLATE HOOPS — 1⅛ Inches broad & as thinn as plate Hoops are, only used in London and the Country round it. They are in length from 5 feet 11 Ins to 12 feet.

PUNCHEON HOOPS — 1⅜ Inches broad, thicker then Coopers Hoops were sent to the West Indies till of late that Coopers Hoops were sent in their place; they are however still sold in London & ordered in lengths 8 to 9 feet long.

BUTT HOOPS — 1½ Inches broad, near as thinn as Coopers Hoops; the common lengths are:
7 feet 2 Inches
7 feet 7 do.
8 feet 0
8 feet 7; some few are 9, 9½, & 10 feet
3 hoops of 10 feet to 2 of any other size.
Crawshay & Compy used to order them of lengths from 7½ feet to 9 feet 2 Inches.

VATT HOOPS — are 2, 2¼, 2½, 2¾, & 3 Inches broad & about ⅛ Inch thick; they are made in lengths from 10 to 24 feet long.

ROD IRON

N. 0	large 3/16th wide	none of these sizes used in London.
1	1¼ wide	
2	5/16th wide	
3 near	⅜ wide	
6	7/16 wide	
8	½ Inch wide	
9	⅝ wide	
11	⅞ wide	
13	1⅛ wide	
20	1½ wide	

The above are Cutt to any thicknes sgenerally all under the N. 9 is Cutt Square.

LETTER REPORTING SUPPLY OF IRON FROM RUSSIA 1804

This letter from a firm of export agents at St Petersburg gives a good picture of the difficulties involved in the purchase of iron and also explains why British iron masters gave up using Russian iron about the beginning of the nineteenth century.

St. Petersburg the 25th Novbr. 1804.

Messrs Wm Cadell Sons & Co.

Sirs, We wrote you last the 21st Ulto with B/L [bill of lading] & Invoice of 302 Bars Iron pr Martha, Primrose m. [master] of Ro 1188.28 & waited on you with Abstract of your account Currt for the balance of which we drew on you at the usual Ro 1821.—Exche 30⅝d.

We since requested our London House to inform you that the Martha was unfortunately caught by the Ice in our river before she could drop down to Cronstadt & in consequence must passe the Winter here.

Our Shipping Season being at an end, we seize an early opportunity of communicating to you a few particulars concerning the exportation of Iron during the year 1804—together with some remarks on the present situation of this Branch of our Trade; We accompany them with a note of the quantity of this article on the spot and expected in May & June 1805, which tho' not quite accurate will assist us in forming a fair judgement of what next year may bring.

The astonishing diminution in the Export of Iron to Great Britain which has taken place in the short space of one year cannot fail of exciting much attention, and this diminution is rendered the more remarkable from its having occurred at a period when our Iron Masters were convinced that the demand must be more brisk than usual in consequence of the droughts we have for two seasons announced & which they had persuaded themselves would produce effects abroad in the prices of Russia Iron not less certain than the failure of the Crop of Rye or other article of universal Consumption must have wrought at home. In persons whose eyes have been shut to the late improvements in England this conviction is natural enough but to such as are no strangers to the amelioration of the quality & the great increase in the quantity of English Iron lately effected, the consequence we now witness must cause less matter for surprise.

At the same time we cannot avoid viewing a falling off in one season of nearly four fifths of the export to the United Kingdoms as too considerable to be the natural consequence even of the high prices here or the Improvements on your side of the water; and as at all events a certain supply of good Russia Iron is yet requisite in England, it becomes a question worthy of enquiry, whether the quantity shipped this year be sufficient for the consumption, and if not whether the advance in price such an event must cause with you may not induce our proprietors here to raise their demand notwithstanding that they will know that Iron which fetches in England £22 pr Ton will barely clear itself if bought at 160 co p pood Exchange 30d.

We have turned this matter in our minds maturely and are pretty well convinced that provided only a moderate advance take place in England, the proprietors of mines here will be willing for some time to come to sell at the prices they have lately demanded. We are of this opinion from reflecting how severely almost all of them have suffered from holding their Iron at prices which the English market could not afford, having thereby been obliged to borrow money at an enormous rate of Interest in order to carry on their works: the most obstinate will now we conceive be sufficiently well pleased if they sell on the terms they have for so long contended for, and some we think might even be persuaded to abate a trifle were an offer made them before an advance in England became generally known here. From a personal acquaintance with the majority of our proprietors we have reason to believe this opinion not unfounded— we would therefore recommend strongly early orders; & as the pecuniary wants of these Gentlemen will naturally render purchases for ready money or with considerable advances the most agreeable to them, such therefore are likely to be the most advantageous to you; & should you favour us with your Commands we shall know how to turn this Circumstance to good Account.

Much indeed must depend on our Exchange, & on this point it is difficult to form any judgement. Besides the question of Exchanges resolves itself into a question of politicks on which we are not capable of deciding were it prudent to discuss it—but if we must express our opinion we should be induced to expect a decline rather than an advance in our Courses.

We could have wished to have been able to name to you the prices demanded by our principal Fabricants, but it is yet too early to expect that their final resolutions can be taken. We hear however that Ivan Jacovleff offers to sell Worontzeff's & Gleboff's N.S. and Silvinsky & Rjevsky at 175 co and his Old Sable at 180 co all with long payments: for his Tyres he expects 175 co money.

For Twerdisheff's common Bar 170 co are demanded & 230 co for the assorted.

The proprietor of Best Gurieff's N.S. has not yet resolved to accept 170 co if offered him.

200 co are asked for CCND and 195 co for PSI, 160 co for Sherayeffs and 170 co for Luginin's.

We shall not fail to wait upon you again whenever any thing interesting occurs, in the meantime we respectfully remain

Sirs

Your most obedient Servants
Thorntons Bayley & Co.

PROFIT AND LOSS AT CRAMOND 1847-60

The books were balanced at Cramond on 30 June each year. The figures given below are those for the preceding year. They do not give any idea of the Company's annual turnover. In fact this information is only given twice. In 1847 it was about £14,000 and in 1850 the exact figure is given, £14,037:11s. The second column includes standard charges such as rents, interest on debts, etc., a sum for wear and tear, and a sum for transport.

	Credit	Debit	Profit/Loss
1847	£3241:19: 7	£1926: 5: 5	+£1315:14: 2
1848	£2398: 9: 8	£1345:17: 4	+£1052:12: 4
1849	£1584: 6: 4	£1259:19: 3	+ £324: 7: 1
1850	£1830: 3:10	£1366: 2: 3	+ £464: 1: 7
1851	£2137:10:11	£1392:17: 1	+ £844:13:10
1852	£2214:19:11½	£1714: 4: –	+ £500:15:11½
1853	£3410:19: 9	£1259: –: 6	+£2151:19: 3
1854	£3579: 8:10	£2497: 1:11	+£1082: 6:11
1855	£3074: 7: 2	£3444:19: 1½	– £370:11:11½
1856	£5450: 9:10	£4646: 9:11	+ £803:19:11
1857	£5014:10:11	£4235:10:10	+ £779: –: 1
1858	£2832:17:11½	£2686:18: 2½	+ £145:19: 9
1859	£2311:18: 2	£2193:12: 1	+ £118: 6: 1
1860	£2418: 2: 9	£4161: 3: 4	–£1743: –: 7

The considerable loss in 1855 was the result of the installation of the new steam engine which necessitated a long break in production. The loss in 1860 is due simply to the general running down of the works.

Losses were mainly incurred in what is called 'manufactured iron', steel, nails and chains. Bar iron was the product which maintained the company's credit. Bar iron was wrought iron refined but still in bar form and should not be confused with what was called bar iron in the eighteenth century, the bars of pig iron such as were imported from Russia. Paper and spades both occasionally went into the red although they account for only a very small part of the company's

output. The curious thing is that Cramond persisted in the manufacture of steel to the end although throughout the whole of this
period it never once made a profit.

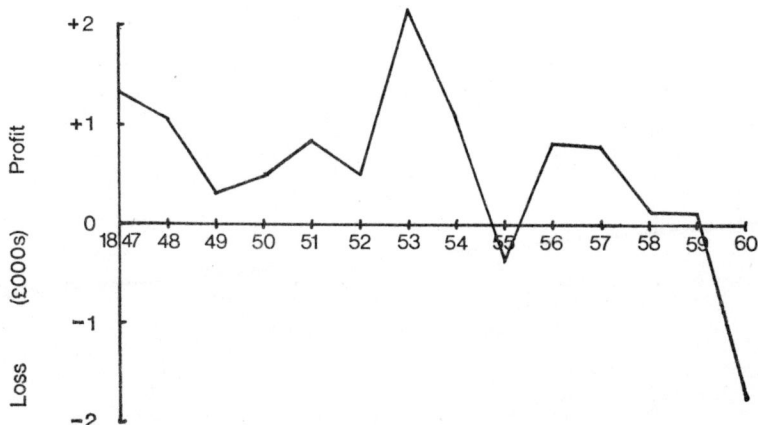

Production figures are not always as clear, and there is always some
doubt as to what is one year's produce, and what has been counted in
from stock made the year before. The following figures seem to be
correct:

	Finished Iron and Forgings.				Spades and Shovels.	Paper.			
1846	1164 tons	7 cwt	1 qu	5 lbs.	1832 doz.	71 tons 16 cwt			
1847	1000	13	–	19	1380	48	10		
1848	1022	3	1	5	1200	44	6		
1849	827	15	2	14	911	45	16		
1850	867	7	3	17	722	20	6		
1851	912	4	3	4	645	51	7	1 q 6 lbs.	
1852	1023	16	2	2	277½	69	10	1	5
1853	1155	9	3	4	188	no figures.			
1854	1151	5	1	–	939	100	6	3	22
1855	1259	13	–	19	913	95	7	3	17
1856	1671	12	–	2	972	113	16	2	16
1857	1666	17	1	14	1037	124	3	–	3
1858	1443	2	2	20	996	103	1	3	5
1859	1568	15	3	25	1004	95	5	–	24

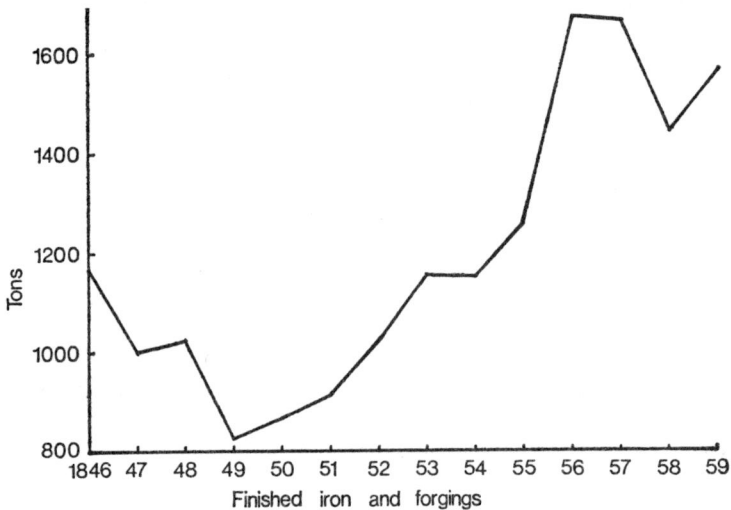

Finished iron and forgings

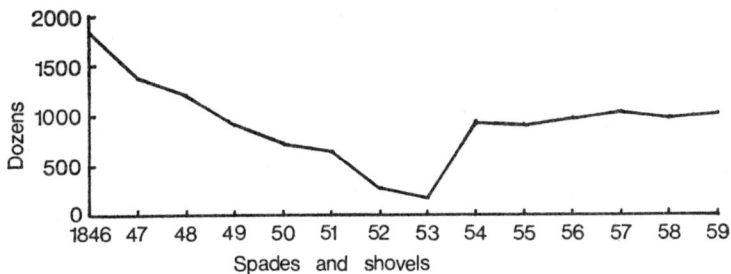

Spades and shovels

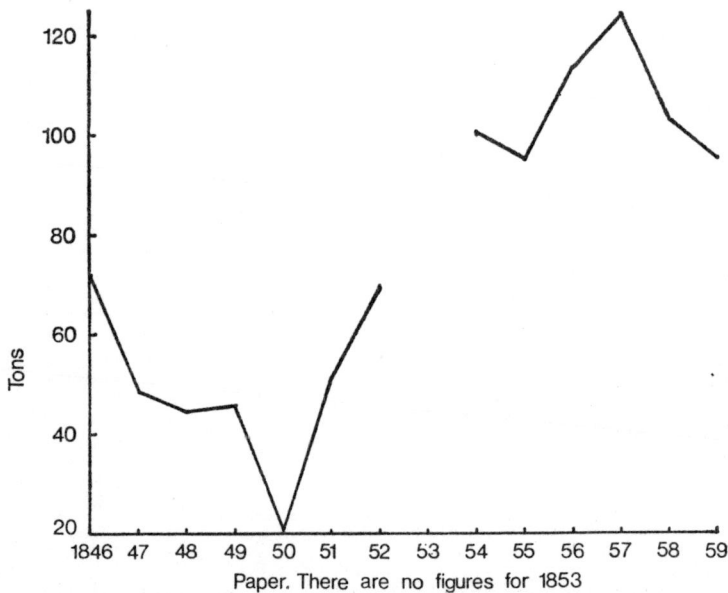

Paper. There are no figures for 1853

LEGAL DISPATCHES INVOLVING CRAMOND IRON WORKS 1774-1852

In the course of its history, the Cramond Iron Works was involved in a number of legal disputes, all of which are interesting as showing the attitudes of outsiders to the activities of the company. They are dealt with here in chronological order.

I

In June 1774 Sir John Inglis obtained an interdict against the Cramond Iron Works preventing the continuation of its improvements to the Fairafar dam which it had undertaken. The cause of Sir John's objections to the improvements was that when the iron works had first been operated at Cramond they had been confined to the lowest mill, while Fairafar had remained a corn mill and waukmill as before. But in the intervening years there had grown up the new vogue for estate improvements, and a new iron mill on the doorstep was not classed as an improvement. In any case the matter was soon decided in favour of the company, as William Cadell remarked to his lawyer on 1 August 1775, 'It is agreeable that the Questions at Fairafar are so far agreeably determined as to allow the work to be compleated, & I hope we shall have Sentence against Sir John for the Expences we have actually paid, if not for the loss & damages we have sustained.'

II

The most serious court action which Cramond ever had to face was that brought by the Earl of Rosebery in 1787. Like Inglis, he was involved in the improvement of his property to which the activities of the Cramond Company were a constant menace. His claim against the company consisted of four main points.

1. He objected to the use of the west bank of the river as a towpath. According to himself the tidal waters of the Almond were not navigable in the strict sense, because they had only been rendered so by the

clearing out of the bed of the river, and therefore they were only to be used by Cramond if it were possible to do so without using the banks. It was alleged that people living in Cramond remembered seeing boats being poled up to Cockle Mill. In addition a wall which at one time ran right down the west bank into the water had been damaged by the men who towed the boats. The use of his land for a towing path is described in the legal memorial as 'a servitude . . . which lays open his [Lord Rosebery's] whole pleasure grounds to the freedoms and devastations of sailors and other disorderly persons employed by the defenders in hauling their boats.'

The defenders alleged that the west side of the river had been used from time immemorial as a way of getting from King's Cramond to the west side of the Coble by way of Cockle Mill dam and the re-building of this dam had been specifically approved by the Earl of Rosebery in 1752 to the extent of his having provided stone for the work. The bottom of the river had been cleared out in the years after 1755 without any apparent opposition. In any case the bank on the east side was too steep to be convenient for towing. As for the remark about pleasure grounds, the company observed, 'In fact . . . the grounds in question have not the smallest appearance of being pleasure grounds. Towards the shore at least, they are in a state of nature, extremely coarse and unpolished.'

This was undoubtedly a matter on which the Earl felt strongly. On one occasion he even went as far as to cut one of the tow ropes himself.

2. Lord Rosebery alleged that the fishing on the Almond had been seriously impaired by the mills, first by the erection of dams that made it impossible for the fish to get up the river, and secondly that even if they were able to get up, they were caught on the way down again by the grates which the mills placed across the entrances to the mill leads. He went as far as to say that Cramond employees had been seen pulling salmon out of these grates. The reply to this was that the fishing was trivial and yielded nothing. In any case the fishing had been ruined before the arrival of the iron works by the pollution of the water caused by the lint steepers higher up the river. Besides there must always have been grates across the mill leads to prevent the machinery from getting clogged up, and no one had previously complained of the removal of fish in this way.

3. Lord Rosebery held that the new dam at Fairafar threw water back on the mill at Craigie. The old dam had been partly of wood on the Dalmeny side and partly of stone and had been so low that there had been stepping stones across the river not very much above

it. The Company stated that the dam had been repaired in 1774 and that Rosebery had only objected in 1775 when his support had been enlisted by Sir John Inglis. In 1780 there was a flood bringing down shoals of ice, which had broken the dam on the Rosebery side by dragging out the metal posts which clamped the dam to the rock and at the same time bringing down part of the river bank. The company had repaired the dam but Rosebery held that it had been repaired to a greater height than before. The fact was, as far as one can see, that the previous dam though built of stone was an ineffective construction. After having advanced several testimonies to the effect that the present dam was no higher than the old one, the company observed, 'The inference in law, that because the Fairyfar damhead was formerly ill constructed, being an irregular heap of stones, it should, now that it is well constructed, be restored to its former bad condition, is certainly one of those novelties in point of claim with which the present process so much abounds.'

4. Finally Lord Rosebery alleged that repairs to the dam at Dowie's Mill had caused a greater flow of water against the haugh land opposite the mill, and that his land was consequently being damaged. The answer to this was that the company had not touched the dam at Dowie's Mill and that any claim of damages in this respect should be made to the representatives of Lady Glenorchy who had been the last person to do anything to the dam.

It seems that these allegations on the part of the Earl of Rosebery were mainly rather trivial, and as far as the Earl was concerned the winning of the case would have given him little except a slight increase in privacy as the company's memorial says, '. . . it cannot fail to have been remarked by your Lordships, that however trifling the objects are which he could promise to obtain, even from the most successful termination of the present suit, they are of the greatest possible consequence to the memorialists; and that if their dams were opened for Saturday slaps [occasional opening of sluices in the dams themselves to allow the passage of fish] and reduced to the ruinous condition which the noble pursuer seems to require, the towing path shut up, and the navigation impeded, or even a small part of this inflicted upon the memorialists, they would be under the absolute necessity of abandoning their extensive works and prosperous manufacture, and of forfeiting that vast expense which has been required to bring them to their present condition.'

The case seems to have been decided out of court. No judicial decision seems to have survived and as Cramond Company remained in business it can only be assumed that nothing was put in its way.

III

Another dispute involving the Cramond Iron Works which very nearly appeared in the courts was with a certain Robert Porter. In May 1836 Porter had agreed to come to Cramond to carry out certain modifications and to introduce certain processes by which the quality of the iron made from scrap was to be improved. The agreement was that Porter would furnish plans for the work and would keep an eye on it but that the day to day supervision of the work would be under the control of his father Robert Porter senior. The Porters were to obtain suitable workmen and in return were to get half the saving and half the additional price the iron might obtain as a result of its improved quality. This was to be calculated over the course of the succeeding calendar year starting from May 1836.

The two big expenses at the Cramond Iron Works, apart from the raw material and wages, were waste iron and coal. It was these that Porter hoped to reduce. There were two furnaces at Fairafar, a ball furnace and a scrapping furnace. Previously it had always been necessary to stop the scrapping furnace while the heats in the ball furnace were being drawn. Porter's plan was to keep both going. In point of fact there seems to have been little to choose between these two methods. The former caused less waste metal because there was no interruption in the drawing of the heats in the ball furnace, while the need to stop the scrapping furnace meant that more coal was required to bring it back up to heat again. In Porter's plan the situation was reversed, more waste but less coal.

It is clear, however, that things did not go well. Old Porter spent most of the summer of 1836 pulling down and repairing the furnaces while his son seems to have been at the works only rarely. When he was there he seems not to have got on with the workmen, both the old workmen and the new ones imported from England. The obtaining of these workmen had been a very expensive business and the company held that much of what little success attended Porter's activities was due not to his new methods but to the skill of the new workmen. There must have been quite an influx at that time. The accounts of work performed for Porter include the following English names, Gaunt, Rabone, Sanson, Hussey, Davis, Picken, and Skidmore. One of the company's complaints was that the payment that Porter claimed was based on work performed by the most skillful workmen of all, Gaunt and Davis.

It is very difficult to see the exact rights and wrongs of the case. Neither side trusted the other: neither was satisfied with the other's trials. The Company held that Porter should pay for the workmen he himself had engaged: Porter claimed he was not responsible for them when the condition of the river had made it impossible for them to work. He also thought that the company had constantly given him short weight in his coal. The result of it all was that Porter claimed he had saved the company £2148 9s 4d, while the company said he had saved them £368 17s 9d. The fact was that while the Company had made a modest profit in the year before Porter's appointment it made a considerable loss while he was there. It is also difficult to see why the company took on someone who was going to do as little as Porter apparently did by way of improving the actual production methods. Once again as with the Rosebery case the matter seems never to have been decided by a court. The arbiters (unnamed) must have come up with some satisfactory solution.

IV

In another bid to improve their production methods the company at one time employed a certain Isaac Hazlehurst who had a special technique for plating iron. There seems to be no record of how successful this method was but it was his 'secret'. After leaving Cramond when he went to be a manager at the Ulverston Iron Works, he claimed that he had sold his secret to no one. He had been employed there partly on the understanding that the secret would be available only to Ulverston. In February 1854 Ulverston dismissed Hazlehurst because they had reason to believe that his secret had already been sold to the Cramond Company. As he was to be tried it was necessary to establish that the secret sold to the Cramond Company was the same as that sold to Ulverston. Henry Cadell was therefore asked whether he would compare the two 'secrets' to see whether they were actually the same. The secret, however, must actually have been a fairly trivial one for Cramond, as Hazlehurst sold it to the company for only £20.

V

Early in 1852 the Edinburgh and Glasgow Railway Company were negotiating a parliamentary bill to enable them as proprietors of the Edinburgh to Glasgow Canal to discontinue their power to take water from the Almond and to cancel their obligation to keep up an average supply of water during the dry summer months from May to October. Under the Canal Act (57 George III cap. 56) the Cramond works were entitled along with the other mill owners to this average flow in the summer in return for the canal company's right to the surplus water in winter. In consideration of this right to an average water supply the Cramond company had spent a considerable amount of money in adapting their machinery to take the maximum advantage of the flow. It did not of course concern the Cramond company that the railway company which now owned the canal would take no more water from the river but they were worried about the threat to the average water supply. They protested for the first time on 22 January 1852. The reply was that as the railway company intended to remove all their works from the Almond they would in fact be restoring the river to its condition before the building of the canal. Hence the Cramond Iron Works could have no possible claim. The matter however was taken up before the parliamentary committee on the bill. The railway company agreed to a settlement before the decision of the committee was actually reached. The Cramond company agreed to a full flow of water until the railway company's works were removed when £1000 would be paid in compensation. In addition the railway company paid £100 for the expenses of the case.

PARTICIPANTS IN THE RESEARCH

Acknowledgment must be made of the work done by Mr Skinner's group in 1965 by:

Mrs Air, Mrs Aitken, Miss Aitken, Mrs Black, Mr Cargill, Mrs Field, Mrs Fraser, Mrs Geddes, Mrs Goldie, Mrs Hanham, Mrs Holmes, Mr Hume, Mr Iggulden, Mr Macfie, Mrs MacIntosh, Miss Pattullo, Mrs Reid, Mr Robertson, Mrs Sclater, Mrs Smith, Miss Stewart.

Mr Cadell's group included:

Mr Aitken, Mrs Black, Miss Bunch, Mr Cowen, Mrs Cowen, Mr Craig, Mrs Craig, Miss Dunnett, Mr Fraser, Miss Gibson, Miss Greig, Mr Hayes, Mrs Hayes, Mrs Honeyman, Mrs Kimm, Mrs MacDonald, Mrs Mackie.

Special thanks are due to Dr J. S. Marshall for information on the Smith and Wright Work Company of Leith and to Sir John Mackay Thomson and W. S. Didcock for information on the two upper mills at various periods. Much assistance has been given at various times during both enquiries by:

Mrs Armstrong (Edinburgh Public Libraries), Professor Michael Flinn (Edinburgh University), Dr Barclay (Edinburgh University), Dr Alastair Thomson (Royal Scottish Museum), Mr Stephen Willy (Ordnance Survey), and above all the staffs of the National Library and the Scottish Record Office.

CADELL FAMILY TREE

Only those members of the family who were in some way or other
involved with the Cramond iron works are included.

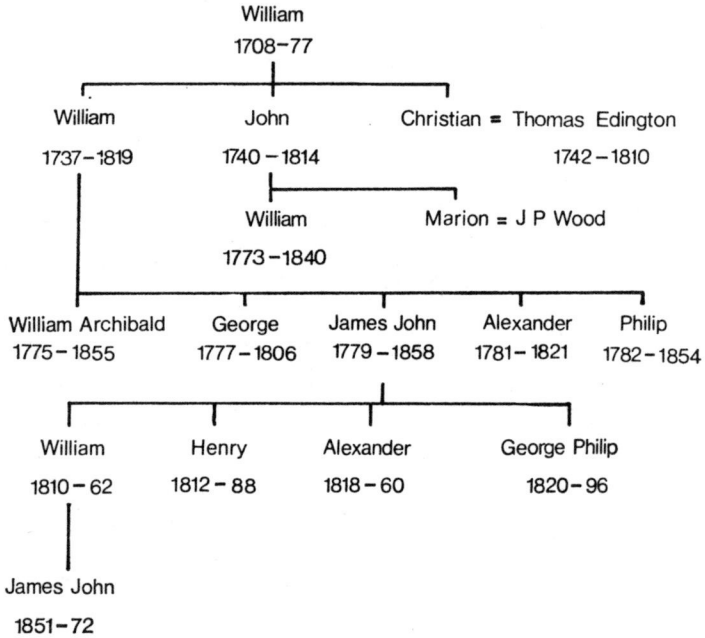

```
                         William
                         1708-77
        ┌──────────────────┼──────────────────┐
     William             John          Christian = Thomas  Edington
    1737-1819          1740-1814                      1742-1810
        │             ┌────┴──────────────┐
        │          William            Marion = J P Wood
        │         1773-1840
    ┌───┴──────────┬──────────┬──────────┬──────────┐
William Archibald  George   James John  Alexander    Philip
1775-1855        1777-1806  1779-1858   1781-1821   1782-1854
   ┌──────────────┬──────────┴──────────────┐
William         Henry      Alexander     George Philip
1810-62        1812-88     1818-60        1820-96
   │
James John
1851-72
```